CELEBRITIES' FAVOURITE PETS

Compiled by Sheila Collins

Foreword by Bob Champion MBE

APEX PUBLISHING LTD

Hardback first published in 2009 by

Apex Publishing Ltd
PO Box 7086, Clacton on Sea, Essex, CO15 5WN, England
www.apexpublishing.co.uk

British Library Cataloguing-in-Publication Data
A catalogue record for this book
is available from the British Library

ISBN HARDBACK: 1-906358-68-0   978-1-906358-68-6

Typeset in 10.5pt Chianti Bdlt Win95BT

Cover Design: Siobhan Smith
Pictures:
Amy Weber with Bella
Edwina Currie with Bruce
Anita Harris with Albert
Linda Lusardi with Koko
Pan & Badger (owned by Emma Milne)
Fluffy (owned by John Challis)
Steve Leonard working in the surgery
Hayley Tamaddon with Ozzy
Indiana Jones (owned by Katherine Kelly)

Printed and bound in Great Britain by the
MPG Books Group, Bodmin and King's Lynn

FOREWORD

I am delighted to write this foreword as having been associated with animals all my life, although mostly with racehorses, I have always cherished the dogs and cats I have had as pets.

My favourite dog was a Jack Russell called "Linney", who was a great character and was definitely a man's best friend.

It is certainly a very different book, and a great insight into other celebrities' favourite pets. It also supports and benefits the PDSA which is a wonderful cause.

Sheila has produced a unique and fascinating book which will make an interesting read for all ages.

Best wishes
Bob Champion MBE

INTRODUCTION

Hi everyone! May I introduce myself as an author and pet lover - but also having the usual British interest in reading about what people in the public eye are up to!

We all in general dote on our pets, so I thought you would like to join with me in reading just exactly what kinds of pets are fortunate enough to live with high-profile celebrities, and why those particular celebrities chose them and love them so much.

One of my own cats, Truffles, became something of a celebrity in her own right with the publication of Truffles' Diaries, which followed her day-to-day activities and comic observations of human behaviour from a cat's point of view, interspersed with humorous anecdotes about past times shared with her many feline and canine friends.

So read on and let your imagination wander into the realm of those lucky pets who are fortunate enough to enjoy lives of luxury - but let's not forget those poor animals who are not so lucky, and this is why a percentage of the sales proceeds from this book will be donated to the PDSA (People's Dispensary for Sick Animals) who work so hard in providing veterinary treatment for needy pets all over the country.

I also want to take this opportunity to say a big thank you to all of the celebrities who have been kind enough to give up some of their time to write about their pets – it is much appreciated, and I hope they will be pleased to see the finished result with, on this occasion, their pets taking centre stage!

Finally, on a personal note, another huge vote of thanks to the staff of Apex Publishing Ltd, in particular Julia and Chris Cowlin, who have gone beyond the call of duty with their work on this book.

Best wishes
Sheila Collins

JENNY AGUTTER
ACTRESS

I can't remember when we acquired our two dogs, Alexandria and Victoria, named after royalty; it seemed they were always there. They were a strange combination of breeds: a highly strung Miniature Poodle, Vicky, and a determinedly naughty smooth-haired Dachshund, Alex. I remember trying to train them, to no avail. They went with us everywhere and were rarely left at our house, which was probably just as well. On one particular occasion I remember the dogs were left home alone. The Dachs managed to open a cupboard in the kitchen in which, amongst other things, there was a bag of flour. By the time we arrived home, both dogs and the entire kitchen were white, coated in a dusting of Homepride! I'm not sure when the cat joined us, but by the time we went to live in Cyprus our feisty black and white cat was a part of the family. He was a smart creature, who just about tolerated the two dogs. We would go for walks and the cat would join us, following on tiptoe behind. Suddenly spying a tree or post, he would rush ahead, climb to a good vantage point and wait for the dogs to pass underneath, whereupon he would leap on the unsuspecting dogs before rushing off, leaving two perplexed animals. Have you noticed that dogs rarely look up?

I have fond memories of these pets; they were there all the time I was growing up. Sadly our cat stayed in Cyprus when we left, as we thought the six-month quarantine imposed at that time would be too much for him. The dogs came back to England and lived to a great age. When I went to live in America my parents wrote to me, and Alex and Vicky were still around and always mentioned in their letters.

BOB ANDERSON
PROFESSIONAL DARTS PLAYER

As a ten-year-old I had a pet rabbit called, almost inevitably, Thumper. He was a real pal. Now, with all the travelling I do, I am unable to have a pet.

KENNY BALL
JAZZ MUSICIAN

We have always had dogs.

At present we have a rescue dog from Florence who is a Doberman/Rottweiler whose name is Farouk. He had been damaged and we paid for him to come over to England. He has Doberman ears, which are straight up and black. He is very obedient but doesn't trust anyone but me and my wife Michelle.

The other dog we have is a German Shepherd called Keyra. She is lovely but looks at you as if you are mad when you tell her off! She is a champion. Her mother and father were both American champions.

The most wonderful dog we have ever had is Sascha. We were going to call her Satchmo but as she was a girl we changed it to Sascha!

FAYE BARKER
NEWS PRESENTER

Mum used to say, "There's no master and dog relationship here - you two are just good mates." She was talking about our Alsatian, Genna, and me, her youngest child.

I first met Genna on the day she was born. I was 7 years old and my stepfather's dog, Gypsy, had given birth to a litter of warm, wrinkly puppies. I watched wide-eyed as the creatures were welcomed into the world, and over the following weeks I would race home from school to play with the six bouncing bundles of joy.

As time passed, people would come to our house and pick which puppy they wanted to take home for their own families and eventually there was only one left. Lucy was the puppy my parents had decided to keep, and she joined her mum, Gypsy, and Suky, our beautiful, glossy black Alsatian, in the chaos that was our family life. Genna, meanwhile, had gone to live with a policeman.

It was over a year later that Mum got a phone call from a local kennels. The lady on the phone told her she thought one of our puppies was there. She was right - it was Genna. Mum brought her back home and I looked in disbelief as this skinny, timid creature walked into the kitchen, cowering if you tried to stroke her. "What's happened to her?" I asked, as Lucy and Suky checked her out too (sadly Gypsy had died that year and was no longer with us). Mum explained that the policeman who bought Genna had decided that she didn't have the 'right nature' to be a police dog, so he had taken her to the guide dogs. But the guide dog training conflicted with what she had been taught as a police dog and it was felt that she wasn't right for that either. She'd then been taken to the kennels - thank goodness the lady there called my Mum.

It couldn't have happened overnight, but I don't ever remember Genna being scared again in our house. She soon learned she was safe and began establishing herself in our pack. She seemed to conclude that the best one to stick with was me - I was the youngest child, she was the newest dog on the block -

and we looked at each other as equals. As Mum said, we became best mates.

As I grew up, Genna was my constant companion. She would be waiting for me as I came off the school bus and, in the summer holidays, we would disappear for hours together in the Devonshire countryside. One day I fell and twisted my ankle. She immediately knew something was wrong and let me lean on her for the short walk home. Another time when I wasn't well she jumped up next to me on my bed, which protested with a loud crack. As I reached my teens she would patiently listen as I told her of my latest adolescent woes, and when I passed my driving test she would try to jump into the back of my Fiesta whenever I went out. One night, when I was 18, I came home very late and was locked out of the house. I managed to climb through a window into the lobby where Genna was waiting, looking at me curiously. The door into the kitchen and the rest of the house was locked, so that night I bedded down with the dogs. They didn't seem to mind but my parents had a bit of a shock when they saw me there in the morning!

When I left home for university my heart would ache saying goodbye to Genna. She now had grey whiskers around her nose and moved a little slower. Suky and Lucy had since passed away and as I said goodbye to Genna at the end of each holiday I dreaded it would be the last.

That awful day came just before I turned 21. Mum didn't know how to tell me as she was worried about how I would take the news, so she wrote a letter and sent it to my student digs in London. It arrived a few days before my 21st and so when I saw it was from my Mum I thought it must be something to do with my birthday ... so I didn't open it straight away. As I came of age on 14th March I reached for my birthday cards, deciding to open the letter from Mum first.

"Now darling," she wrote, "something we didn't tell you. Dear old Genna had to be put down a week ago ... the vet was very good but said nothing could be done ... but she had a good life."

It wasn't unexpected but it hurt all the same, and on the day I reached adulthood I mourned the loss of my childhood companion. I still miss Genna dearly, but those fabulous memories of our time together and the image of her bright smiling eyes keep her alive in my heart.

ALLY BEGG
SPORTS BROADCASTER

I'm going to start with a bold statement: my black Labrador Casper is without doubt the finest K9 Scotland has ever produced.

At the time of writing, Casper, or 'The Wee Man' as he's fondly known to his many adoring fans, is four years old but still possesses the energy of a young pup. I bought him from a small farmstead near Loch Lomond in Scotland; he was the only male dog left, surrounded by his faithful sisters who were keen to remain siblings. As we drove back into Glasgow my partner at the time, Abbie (Casper's Mum), held him close to her chest for the duration of the journey and an instant love affair began.

That evening we did our best to build him a small pen in the spare room of our apartment, but to no avail; Casper cried the place down. Guilt-ridden, I gave in and allowed him to sleep with us in our bedroom - he slept soundly above Abbie's head on her pillow! Over the coming months we discovered we had bought a little gem. He was house trained within weeks, never caused a fuss with his food and greeted visitors as though they were long lost friends. He loves the company of people and has no hesitation in letting them know that.

Like many Labradors he lives for his ball, and he's at his happiest in the park surrounded by many trees upon which to relieve himself at his own leisurely pace. The energy that he exhibits as he runs back and forth gleefully with said tennis ball in his frothy mouth has no boundaries. He would happily run all day given the opportunity. Not one to show his boldness when confronted by other dogs, Casper submits quite sheepishly, hence the reason he still has his 'balls'. Chop those babies and a serious case of bullying could be on the cards. When confronted he merely puts his head to one side and then proceeds to lie on his back and wag his tail!

One of Casper's favourite pastimes is to swim, be it in Loch Lomond, the sea or large puddles. After we moved to Singapore we took Casper to the beach as often as possible. On Sentosa Island, just south of Singapore, is a designated beach for people with dogs. The beautiful white sands surrounded by lush palm trees and a mind-blowing lagoon make it a hot spot for locals and ex-pats alike. He likes nothing more than having his ball thrown as far out into the lagoon as possible, especially if one of us is in there with him. On a particularly hot day it was my turn to swim out into the lagoon as Abbie threw the ball back and forth. Now, to give you an idea of Casper's toilet habits, he is like no ordinary dog taking a number 2! At first he will break into a small jog, running back and forward searching for the right spot and then, instead of using his nose to sniff out the area, he uses his bottom, spinning on a sixpence with tail flailing behind him until he is satisfied the position has been secured before he proceeds to do you know what. This must be done on the finest piece of grass that Singapore has to offer, so imagine our horror when after a few minutes at the beach the dreaded jog began along the shoreline!

As I was a good 20 metres out into the lagoon treading water, I was in no position physically to do anything. As the glazed look in Casper's eyes washed over him the spinning began and the line "dropping the kids off at the pool" could not have been more appropriate at this time. Abbie in the meantime was paralysed to the spot, not quite taking in what was unfolding, and began howling at me, "He's having a poo, he's having a poo!"

All I could do was swim to shore and try in the coolest way possible to collect the small items of brown pellets in a plastic bag as the waves washed them ashore one by one. If there had been a hole anywhere on that beach I would have gladly climbed into it - the shame was too great for one to bear. Not that Casper was oblivious to the carnage he had just created, but he was back in the lagoon swimming happily for his ball!

Living in Singapore with Casper has been an odd experience. He is undoubtedly the most popular dog where I currently live, happily engaging everybody with his dumb smile and the uncontrollable shake of his body that eventually finds its way to his tail. But, in saying that, he is also loathed by some - jumping out the way or going rigid with fear as if the devil himself is about to be unleashed on them. I understand it's due to a cultural and partly religious belief that dogs are seen as dirty and not to be approached. I personally have no understanding or patience with such drivel, as all Casper wants to do is merely be everybody's friend. I look forward to the day when I can return to Scotland and allow the shores of Loch Lomond to be used as his playground once again.

LORNA BENNETT
ACTRESS

My Uncle Bernard's dog, Rupert, was a favourite pooch of mine with a natural penchant for the stage. If he wasn't dressing up as an old maid (now I come to think of it, Uncle Bernard may have had a hand in his donning the glasses/headscarf/shawl combo), he was stealing someone's spotlight.

Rupert's top telly moment came during the mid-eighties, in Sherwood Forest, when he interrupted a reverential recording of Blue Peter (on the subject of Robin Hood, naturally) by running up to Mark Curry, who was perched artistically on the Merry Men's Great Oak Tree, and promptly piddling on them both.

Truly a Favourite Celebrity Pet.

DAVE BENSON PHILLIPS
CHILDREN'S TV PRESENTER, ENTERTAINER
& BROADCASTER

When I was a young boy I had a chubby, brown, stripy cat called Teeoffalus (pr. TEE-OFF-AL-US).

We called it such a curious name because we were not sure of the cat's gender, so we gave the cat an extremely unique name. It was not until we found Teeoffalus with a litter of kittens in a box under my dad's workbench, that we realised Teeoffalus was a she! Dad wanted to rename the cat 'Sheoffalus' in recognition of her gender ... but we all thought that was a silly name for a cat. So Teeoffalus remained her name for a very, very long time.

JULIA BRADBURY
TELEVISION PRESENTER

They say a dog needs a master, but Lotte doesn't have one; she has many and they are mostly mistresses. A black Miniature Schnauzer, she was bought principally for my nephew, Jack, as an easygoing hound. Schnauzers are famously even-tempered and they don't moult. Jack wanted one because of a cartoon dog called Lotte that he'd fallen for. She's a funny, scatty little thing, and because we as a family are often on the move she stays with all of us at some time or another. She has her own little routine in each home - with Mum and Dad she has a doggy beanbag that she loves.

When she's staying with me she always escapes from the garden and heads out to run wild through the neighbours' gardens. She doesn't have the standard Schnauzer haircut (a little 'man-beard') - instead she sports a shaggy do. The women in the family are of Greek descent and so we've all got thick, wildish hair - just like her!

JO BRAND
COMEDIENNE

I grew up with cats, we always had one – and since we lived in fairly rural places I think I can say our cats had a good life. Me and my brothers took ownership of one or other as they came, and sometimes went, but always it was my mum who dealt with the tins or cooking up some seriously smelly 'titbit' from the butcher.

After a long cat-free break we have a feline presence in our house, and in ever increasing numbers – currently four, one with a brood, who were not really invited or expected, but we've found them all 'good homes'.

Their individual personalities are an absorbing distraction from household chores, answering e-mails and contemplating my navel. I am fond of them all. I admire their self-possession and self-assurance, from total indifference to suddenly seeking my undivided attention – sounds a bit like my husband! Make that five 'cats' then, and my children are much the same, so make that seven!

I'm a martyr to the culinary predilections of my entire household!

No doubt I will have cats well into my dotage - the two of us will take off with a caravan in tow, park up on the hardcore of some convenient poet or wit and enjoy a little luxuriant laziness - well, that's my fantasy. Long Live Cats!

GYLES BRANDRETH
WRITER, BROADCASTER
& FORMER MP

Many years ago we had two cats, Oscar and Thornton. (Oscar was wild; Thornton was worse.) Oscar ate Spot, our children's beautiful pet goldfish, and at the memorial service (we couldn't have a funeral: there were no mortal remains - Oscar scoffed the lot) I recited this poem, now officially the Shortest Poem in English Literature. It is called "Ode to a Late Lamented Goldfish". (The title is longer than the poem. Read it slowly. It rhymes. It is a traditional poem. And now, I am proud to say, regarded as a bit of a classic.) Here it is - "Ode to a Late Lamented Goldfish" by Gyles Brandreth:

O
Wet
Pet!

GEOFF CAPES
FORMER BRITISH SHOT-PUT CHAMPION & FORMER WINNER OF 'THE WORLD'S STRONGEST MAN'

My favourite pets are my budgerigars, as I compete at shows throughout the country and it keeps my competitive instinct alive. I would, however, keep them as pets, as I think that birds are wonderful and there are so many different colours to look at now whereas the original colour was just green.

JOHN CHALLIS
ACTOR

Our cat, Fluffy. When we arrived at our current home, eleven years ago, we inherited seven farm cats! Fluffy is the daughter of a feral black/orange/white mother and a visiting grey father. She had one litter of her own, six kittens, and she would lead them through the long grass in a 'crocodile' line from one safe place to another. She has an enormous long tail and very furry black legs with black 'boots' and is always trailing leaves and brambles.

Her cousin, Mortimer, a black and white tom, catches mice and small rabbits and Fluffy will often do a flying bypass and snatch the kill from his mouth.

When she was young Fluffy would not come anywhere near us or the house, but now she is older she wanders into the kitchen and rolls over by the Aga. But she will not let us touch her. Her two daughters, whom we gave to one family in the village and another right down in Dorset, were both given the name Abby – and, coincidentally, a son was called Wiggy – all named after Fluffy's home.

Fluffy gives us so much pleasure and is always somewhere nearby with Mortimer when we are in the garden. Long may they both hunt and be happy!

ERROL CLARKE
ACTOR

Hi, my name is Errol Clarke - and apart from sounding like an intro to an AA meeting, I am an actor! I, like most people, have changed my tastes as I've grown older. I still love most animals, but now have fish as my desired choice of pet.

I'm not sure if you can officially call them pets, but they do keep me happy. Their habitat isn't quite a massive tank, but then they are not exactly big!

I got them originally as I thought that I would see if I could look after them and not kill them! Maybe it was a bit shallow, but I also thought that maybe it would be cheaper and would need less responsibility, and not be as inhumane as if I had bought something larger. I am not downplaying fish, but it's not as if they are like other domesticated creatures.

As an actor, time is never your own, unless you can afford to make the time. I enjoy doing the work I do, as it's living all my dreams at once. I wanted to be a world-class athlete and judoka when I was younger and almost got enough medals to sate my ambition, but on leaving the RAF after 12 years as an aircraft mechanic I ended up becoming an actor!

I think, given the amount of time spent acting, the fish is the easiest creature for me to look after and it's very therapeutic. I haven't given them names, as they all look similar, and I am no expert on fish yet either, but they seem to fit my lifestyle and commitment level at this moment. Hopefully I will be able to upgrade to bigger tanks and fish when I become more confident and knowledgeable about each fish and their requirements ... and become richer, of course!

I have a few projects in the pipeline for TV and film and have films completed yet to be released and look forward to their progress. Then I will be able to afford another fish tank! I hope that when the next publication comes out, and if I'm allowed to, I should be at a point in time where I will have made additions and upgraded my current level.

Thank you for taking the time to read about my fish and keep smiling.

SHEILA COLLINS
AUTHOR & COMPILER

I have had many pets in my life. I grew up as a young child with two cats, a rabbit and a budgie, and when I was about eleven or twelve a golden Cocker Spaniel pup, Brandy, arrived. My friend Heather and I arrived at my home for tea one day to find this tiny, chubby, adorable little creature curled up in a little basket on the hearth. I loved him madly but I have to admit it was really my Dad who looked after him! When six years later I moved away to flat-share in London, Brandy remained at home with my Dad and was a great companion to him as my parents were divorced by that time. Brandy lived to nearly 18 years of age.

Fast forward several more years and, living in Cornwall, we had (though not all at the same time!) seven cats of assorted shapes, colours and sizes, a couple of hamsters (who didn't appreciate cats peering at them in their safe haven of a cage, so they were found new homes), a Basset Hound, a St Bernard, a Macaw and various birds of smaller sizes, plus indoor tropical and outdoor fish. As many of the contributors to this book have stated, it is very difficult to have a favourite pet. I loved them ALL but my 'past favourite', I suppose, has to be Tansy – a little black and white long-furred rescue kitten who stole our hearts and was as endearing when she grew up as she was when we first saw her at just 5 weeks old. She was always very small – the vet said her mother had probably had a teenage pregnancy and so must have been small herself! We originally had intended to get one kitten and I had already spotted Truffles, a gorgeous tabby kitten, who I had immediately decided upon. However, her tiny black and white pal was just as irresistible, so we left with the two of them! Tansy was always in trouble – as those of you who have read my books, Truffles' Diaries, will know (for example, jumping into a large bowl of trifle when we were holding a smart garden party!) She was so cute, though, that whatever scrapes she got into she knew she'd always be cuddled and forgiven! She had the art of 'cuteness' down to a tee!

When last year I lost the sole survivor of the above-mentioned pets, Truffles, my literary cat, aged nearly 20, I thought I would try to stay pet-free for at least a year – no ties, travel, freedom! But after only three months, it was just no good - once a pet lover, always a pet lover! So now I have my 'latest favourite' pet – a sweet little grey and white cat called Misty whom I got from Cat Protection. She had had a pretty miserable start to life and was extremely nervous, but within days - after kindness and a certain degree of patience - she settled in and has turned into a loving companion always ready for a chat and a cuddle. She is a very 'girly' cat. She never goes out in wet or windy weather, her fur is always immaculate, and she has a wardrobe of pale pink collars to match her nose (!). Everybody who sees her says, "Oh, isn't she pretty!" ... Pity nobody's ever said that to her owner!

NAT COOMBS
COMEDIAN, WRITER & TV PRESENTER

I think it's an impossible task to pick a favourite pet – "each is outstanding in its own way" to steal a line from the movie Animal House - though I suspect that Rocky, a roguish King Charles Spaniel that I spent most of my formative years chasing, or apologetically collecting from neighbours, would probably have tried disreputably to fix it to ensure I chose him.

But it's an undoubted soulmate of Rocky's that I've decided to write about. The Count arrived in our lives a few years ago. Some would say he's a cat, but his remarkable appearance evokes a variety of animals, including, in no particular order – a fruit bat, a spider monkey and a wild owl. His expression is one of permanent surprise – wide, orange eyes that stare at you inquisitively. He has long, jet black, messy fur that is shocked up in a remarkably uncoordinated manner and his general gait is one of ambivalent coasting, as if he's taking a mid-morning saunter through a sunny park, irrespective of his location.

Despite an undoubtedly good heart, he's certainly fond of the finer things in life. My wife and I are convinced he runs a neighbourhood card game and I'm certain that when he disappears under the bed I can hear strains of Sinatra and mini-cubes of ice being dropped into a whisky tumbler. We once got a phone call for him from a lady named Candy, a breathless individual who didn't leave a forwarding number and just asked us to tell The Count that she'd see him in Reno.

Of course, he's incredibly noisy, and decides he's going to engage in loud, one-way dialogue at random times of the day, more often than not in the early hours. His fellow feline housemates seem to find him an affable sort of chap – and I think we all feel that underneath his cavalier approach to life he's a pretty decent pal to have, notwithstanding those occasions when we have to settle his gambling debts.

JUDY CORNWELL
ACTRESS

My first pet was a kitten found in the outback of Australia. Her mother had been killed by a snake. I called her Sooty. She became a devoted pet who would follow me to school in the morning and be waiting for me when I returned. She saved me from a nest of snakes, which I thought was her family of kittens playing in a field. She killed many snakes with the skill of a mongoose and would proudly lay them out underneath my bedroom window.

My second pet was a grass snake I found on the Sussex Downs. I kept him warm in my bedroom for the winter and released him back on the Downs in the summer.

My third pet was a white rabbit I found wet and bedraggled in a street in Hove. I took him home and the next day, while waiting to buy a hutch for him, put him in the number one dressing room of the Dolphin Theatre where I was a student assistant stage manager. The visiting star who turned up for rehearsals let out a scream when confronted by the rabbit in her dressing room, and I thought I was in deep trouble! But she wanted to keep the rabbit in her dressing room all day because that morning she had received news that her great friend Jack Buchanan had died, and the last play they had worked on together had been Harvey the White Rabbit. This was the beginning of a great friendship between this wonderful woman and myself.

My last pet was a Cairn Terrier called Harry Parry. He was chosen by my son from a litter and I loved him. I immortalised him in my first novel, Cow and Cow Parsley. He lived for fifteen years and was a cherished member of the family. I have not had a pet since he died.

EDWINA CURRIE
AUTHOR & FORMER MP

Our dogs are our favourite people. The German Shepherd, Sheba, came to us in March 2005 and just kept growing; she's big, and hairy, but totally beautiful with a lovely nature. Her companion, Bruce, is a rescue dog from Greek Animal Rescue; he's about seven years old we think and shows his true colours whenever dinner is on the table!

Bruce was the name he was given by the ladies of Greek Animal Rescue. His original name is a mystery; maybe he never had one. He's mostly a hound, brown and long-eared, with a daft smile. He was dumped on the rubbish tip in Skiathos in northern Greece, perhaps because he's a dead loss as a hunter. That's because he doesn't understand the phrase "Come back!" in any language. He loves chasing rabbits in the fields near our house in Surrey, but if he caught one it would be a miracle as he makes such a hullabaloo as he streaks across the landscape. Ten minutes and miles later he has completely forgotten where he was supposed to be. Many hours pass before he wearily trudges home. In his sleep his paws are still moving.

Taking in a stray like him demands some courage - a fact we discovered only after he arrived. The charity had chipped, vaccinated, snipped and trained him, up to his limit; he's taken to the easy life and sneaks off to sleep on a sofa, not something allowed to our other dog Sheba (a big Alsatian), who is miffed at this preferential treatment. Outside he has to stay on a lead. But since he knows what hunger is all about, he's a walking stomach.

Bruce could eat for England but is curiously selective. Dog kibble he despises but plain bread is fine; he has obviously begged at many Greek café tables. Tap water doesn't suit but any dirty puddle will do. When we had prawns he got very excited but would only eat the shells and claws, tail wagging. He'll clean up any pan, any dish, dig into any rubbish bin; his eagerness gives my heart a wrench, as he obviously had to do it before just to survive.

What makes him magic is his gratitude. At first reserved with us, even shy, he faithfully puts up with whatever we (and Sheba) ask him to do. She taught him to play, though he has no idea what a stick or ball are for. He is brave: on outings he places himself between us and anything he perceives as a danger. And when he was sick and I nursed him I was rewarded with the tiniest lick from this dog who had never learned to say "thank you" before.

He's a very special person is Bruce. With patience and love he's turned into a great character ... even if he can't be trusted to return when there are rabbits about.

VENDA D'ABATO
ACTRESS (US)

Since my early childhood in South Texas, I have been an animal lover. I was particularly drawn to horses and fish, an odd combination, I know. Growing up, I wanted to be a large animal veterinarian, which was likely due to the influence of my mother, who has always been involved with horses. I was amazed at how gentle our horses were, in stark contrast to how enormous they appeared to a small girl. I felt then, as I do now, that aggression from animals is a reflection of how they are treated by their handlers, and my mother took great care of her horses.

I have also always had a strong attraction to black and white animals, such as penguins, angelfish, and especially zebras. To me, there is something mystical and earthy about zebras. Trying to distinguish the reason for my attraction to colorless animals would be difficult; maybe it has to do with all of the "gray" areas of life.

I've always been drawn to South Africa, and maybe that's the reason for my fascination with zebras. For as long as I can remember, I've felt a life calling to do humanitarian work with AIDS victims in South Africa. When I am able to achieve this, I will have accomplished what is perhaps the biggest goal of my life. Coincidentally, the name Venda, which was given to me by my grandmother, is also the name of a tribe of people in South Africa.

Unfortunately, I don't have a pet zebra, but I have the next best thing; two great dogs named Max and Gaff. Max is the guy in the photos with me; Gaff was being camera shy!

They are more family than my pets. I am humbled by their benevolent nature and I am positive they give more to us than we to them. During times of great stress and despair they have a beautiful way of helping one realize that there is goodness and purity in the world, and remind you to live in the moment.

ANNA EASTEDEN
ACTRESS & MODEL (US)

The most vivid memory from my childhood is when my cat brought in three little kittens. I must have been six or seven years old and my red tabby cat had been lost for a week. That morning I woke up, went to the kitchen and saw my cat through the window walking towards our front door with something in its mouth. I ran outside to open the door for the cat. I noticed she was carrying a tiny kitten in her mouth. I took the kitten from my cat and brought it in. After my cat felt that her baby was safe with me, she wanted to go back outside. I opened the door for her and she left. Five minutes later she came in carrying another baby kitten! I carried this one inside also and the cat went out again. She brought in a third kitten! I felt so proud having been able to help my cat and that my cat trusted me enough to give me her newborn kittens.

MONIQUE EDWARDS
ACTRESS (US)

When I was about twelve or thirteen years old I had a guinea pig named Fred. Fred was an absolute delight from day one. My mother placed her in my lap and the first thing she did was to scoot back as far as she could into my lap and 'mark' me. I was now hers. At the time I had no idea what her scooting back meant. However, I did a quick study and learned that when she started scooting backwards it meant that she was in need of a lavatory.

After a couple of weeks with Fred I discovered that she was not a 'Fred' but a 'Frederica'. Apparently the woman who had given us the guinea pig didn't know that Fred was a 'girl'. I use the word 'girl' because Fred was more human than guinea pig! We thought about changing her name to Frederica but Fred was most definitely a Fred. She was absolutely adorable. She was a long-haired Peruvian guinea with gorgeous camel and white hair and a personality second to none. There were times when she would be sitting in my lap and she would get an urge and literally climb up me so that she could nuzzle in the crook of my neck. The first time she did that she scared the wits out of me. She also had a litter box that she was trained to use. This was great because she didn't have to be caged up all the time. At dinner time, if Fred was out, she was most likely under the table filing down her teeth on our shoes or standing on her hind legs begging for food with that distinct 'whistle' she would let out.

Occasionally Fred would try to sneak into the family room. Sometimes she would make it, unnoticed by us. All we had to do was call her name and she would come tearing back across the floor and jump into her litter box as if to say that she had been there all along. It was actually quite funny. She knew she was in trouble, so she would just look at you with those wonderful eyes and there was nothing you could do. She had us 'wrapped' and she knew it. She was spoilt rotten! In the dead of winter my dad would often go out and clear a patch of snow so that Fred could have fresh grass. He would also go to the grocery store and get different treats for her. She had a cage that I would cover with a towel at night so she wouldn't get too cold - only to find out on more than one occasion that she had used the towel to make her great escape! She would be just sitting there looking at you as if nothing was going on.

We would take her on vacation with us and if the area was clear we would let her roam free. She would get so excited. She would get as low to the ground as she could, as though she were on some kind of reconnaissance mission, and scurry through the grass. She never tried to get out of our reach and when it was time to go we would scoop her up and be on our way.

I could go on but suffice to say she was a wonderful pet and 'friend'. I loved her dearly and I'm pretty sure she loved me too. She lived for 12 years and brought a lot of love and joy into our lives and she is sorely missed to this day.

TAMI ERIN
ACTRESS & MODEL (US)

In my twenties I had a beautiful cat named Squiggie (pronounced Sq-i-j-ee). When I saw her at the pet store it was love at first sight. The very first time I saw her she reached out to touch me. After she climbed around on my shoulders and we played for a few minutes I knew I wanted to take her home.

When we arrived home we laid down on the couch to take a nap. She was so small that I held her in my cupped hands, near my face. After our 'cat nap' I opened my eyes and she opened hers and looked at me … and it was love. The following morning I woke up with her tiny paw stroking my face to wake me up for breakfast.

We were a pair from then on. She slept in my long hair that was made into a nest above my pillow. We ate breakfast together, Eskimo kissed and sang. When I would sing she would meow and that's how we went on for many years.

Her favourite foods were turkey and tuna. She was tiny and black with pretty green eyes and a pink nose. Since she was black, if she was out at night and I couldn't find her I would call out "tuuurrrkeeyyyyyyy" and she would come running from wherever she was. It was extra funny because sometimes people thought my cat was named "tuuurrrkeeyyyyyyy"!

There are not enough words to describe the big love I felt for Squiggie. She was my furry baby, my best friend and my love. Sometimes I think if I were a cat I'd want to be Squiggie, and I think if she were a human she'd want to be me.

ROSIE FELLNER

ACTRESS

(Sprint = to run, to jog, to dash or dart.)

Mine was called Sprint. He was my first dog when I was a child and died a few years ago. To me, a trusted companion and consoling friend who would sit by my side and share my thoughts with his deep steel eyes and loyal demeanour. Sprint, my dog!

CHERYL FERGUSON
ACTRESS

I had a greyhound called Carol. She was gentle and loving and thought she was human – she is sadly no longer with us.

I have a parrot now called Charlie – a very colourful character who asks "What you doing?" every time you eat and drink!

CHRISTOPHER FOSH
ACTOR

My favourite pet was my pure white Boxer called Beau. He was the most gentle and faithful animal I have ever owned.

I got him twelve years ago and I remember picking him up from the breeder: when he appeared from under the sofa where he was hiding, on seeing this white bundle of ill-fitting furry skin, I instantly fell in love with him and knew he was the dog for me! Those baby puppy dog eyes just melted my heart.

From that day on, he was my faithful friend, hardly ever leaving my side. Whenever I went away for work, for however long, he would be sat at the window waiting for me to return, and when I did I was greeted by his wagging stump of a tail and him going nuts to see me again.

He always made me feel loved and it was always unconditional!

I will miss him. Beau passed away in June 2009 after becoming quite poorly and I feel I've lost a part of me. I will never forget the fun times we had. He was my four-legged best friend!

BOBBY GEORGE
PROFESSIONAL DARTS PLAYER

My favourite pets are my dogs. Over the years I have lost a King Charles, two Bearded Collies and a Border Collie. My present dogs are Jack Russells - five of them! My Jacks are named after money – Twopee, Visa, Gilda, Fiver and our baby Cash. They are the most loving of dogs and it never ceases to amaze me how much they love man. We have so much fun with them and they are brilliant hunters!

JANEY GODLEY
COMEDIENNE & WRITER

I loved my crazy, black dog, Major! He was mad! An angry dog, always on the lookout for victims like pigeons or cats! Our backyards were a square set of twenty blocks of flats with open closes that led through to the front streets. All the individual closes had penned-off back yards, which were segregated by green painted railings. Major loved getting into other people's yards.

I would take him out, clipping the thick metal dog leash onto his collar, and be dragged off at speed down all the stairs outside. He would try to pull off the leash to chase imaginary cats. I couldn't let him free as he would bite the first living thing he spotted and I didn't want to get into dog disputes, so I would run around the back letting him sniff bins, scratch at the ground and snuffle through the long grass near the railings. He would look up at me, pleading to be set free – he wanted to run about – but every time I let him go he slipped his bony body through the metal railings and set off on a 'bitefest', and although I was wiry and fast I couldn't climb over those spiky fences and catch up with him. He was an expert escapee. Before I knew it he would be on the main road attacking pensioners and babies! He was mental and very scary looking. "No, Major, you will run off and bite people," I answered as he stared at me.

One day he did get away from me and I saw his tail disappear through the close into the front street from where I could hear screams! My heart was pounding; I was exhausted and sweating. Why did I let him go? I saw an old woman pinned up against a front garden fence with Major barking at her feet, but he spotted me and ran off in the direction of the big main road. Finally he came to a stop. He watched me over his shoulder and sat on the pavement quietly as I approached him stealthily. I fully expected him to bolt off again as I got closer, but he didn't move. "Major, you bad dog!" I shouted as I clipped the leash on him. He just stared at me and padded off quietly.

I had to go to the Co-op and now had the dilemma of how to get into the shop with Major – he couldn't be tied up outside as he would bite folk. The big glass door jangled as I entered. Major growled low in his throat; he hated new places. My dog was rather autistic and anal for a domesticated animal. Things set him off, like a doorbell or a floor brush, and he despised goldfish and fish tanks - he attacked them viciously; he tried to bite the fishbowl in my bedroom. He was mad! Anyway, Major was tied to the big pillar at the side of the counter and eventually, business done, we left.

I spotted the butchers shop on the way home and decided to treat Major to some scraps – he was barred from the shop as he was known for his daring raids when he would run in and try to drag a side of beef off the butcher's hooks! I tied him to the lamp post outside – he wouldn't bite anyone as he could smell the meat in the shop and that thought would occupy his mind.

The butcher smiled as he wrapped up some liver and a huge bone in greaseproof paper - "It's okay, Janey", he said, "no charge for the scraps and keep that crazy dog back from my shop." Major wolfed down the wee bits of liver and chomped on the bone and we both marched home happily. I realised that if Major had a bone in his mouth he would never bite anyone, so maybe we would have to keep him supplied with bones forever?

ANITA HARRIS
ACTRESS, SINGER & ENTERTAINER

Albert, my Afghan, named 'Albert T. Queurkletule' after a fictional eccentric scientist featured in a humorous advertising campaign created by my husband, Mike. Albert was great fun, appeared in over 100 TV shows and gave an unscheduled appearance on stage at the London Palladium! He lived to an age of eighteen and a half years. We loved him dearly.

MARCUS HARRIS
ACTOR

Never work with animals or children. This was probably a sentiment agreed with wholeheartedly by the Southern Television crew working on ITV's Famous Five back in the late '70s. And who can blame them, having to work with four spirited children, me as Julian, Gary Russell as Dick, Jennifer Thanisch as Ann and Michelle Gallagher as George, and of course one fantastic black and white Border Collie called Toddy but known to millions as Timmy, the fifth member of the Five.

Toddy played his part heroically in the show, returning unbelievable distances through dank tunnels in order to sound the alarm, disarming burly men with guns, digging furiously to free a stranded child stuck behind a rockfall or simply holding off the baddies with a volley of aggressive woofing that seemed so out of place for such a placid dog. Such was the training and professionalism of Toddy Woodgate.

My pet life at that time, however, wasn't all plain sailing. Being away from home for the best part of two years, I never really noticed how my own dog, a rough Collie called Cheppie, had grown old. He had arrived in our home a few months before I was born and, rather like me, was always a mischievous pup; as we grew up together we were in a sense partners in naughtiness. I recall being summoned home from school one day as Cheppie had tried to scramble out of an upstairs window that he shouldn't have been able to reach and got stranded woofing heroically halfway in and out, much to the amusement and consternation of the assembled neighbours. My mother was out doing the shopping, so at age 12 I was the one to perform a daring rescue before returning to school a hero.

Coming home then one Friday evening during the second year of filming, tired and as usual mentally stuck somewhere between my two worlds, to be sat down by my parents and told that Cheppie had died was devastating. They waited until they could tell me face to face and not over the phone, which is something I have always been grateful for.

For the rest of the series Toddy was a great comfort - to still have a dog who was, on some level, partly mine eased a lot of grief but made it even harder when The Famous Five finished. Having lived like a family for two years, sharing a house with the other children, seeing and playing with Toddy each day, it all seemed very abrupt. Gary, Jennifer, Michelle and I stayed in touch but regrettably I never got to feed Toddy a sausage again. It was in a sense my second lost dog.

As I grew into an adult the memory of Toddy was never far away. Frequently I would leave a pub to a rousing chorus of the series theme tune, 'We are the Famous Five'. The majority of drunken revellers, not really knowing the lyrics, would stumble along until the last line 'and Timmy the do-oo-oog', which was usually sung amidst much hilarity. The other witty and frequently original retort was, "Which one were you then? Timmy the dog?", again accompanied by much laughter. In this and many other ways I have never forgotten him.

It was perhaps then no surprise as a married man with two young boys both desperate for a dog that we came away from Stadhampton Rescue Centre with the most amazing Collie called Kerwyn. The funny thing was I never thought of the similarity with Toddy until somebody else pointed it out. Surely the mind works in mysterious ways. He instantly took to our home and has become a much-loved part of the family. Even after my marriage broke down we still found a way of sharing Kerwyn, which means I get him at weekends. Without any detriment to Toddy, Kerwyn is, if anything, slightly brighter than the original and entertains with an impressive series of acrobatic manoeuvres, all performed without the aid of a safety sausage.

During the recent filming of an interview to celebrate 50 years of Southern Television, Jennifer and I were reunited to reminisce on camera about our time in the Five. Kerwyn came along as a prop dog, and, whilst I think they cut his big scene, he served as a very able stand-in for Timmy.

My new partner, however, has a penchant for Orange Dogs, and after we lost her much loved but very ill ten-year-old Vizsla called Alfie we adopted Albert. Albert is the very opposite of Kerwyn; where the Collie is bright Albert is cute. Those of you who know Vizslas will recognise him from the photos, but for those that don't he is a Wire Haired Vizsla with a perfect orange tuft on the top of his head and whiskers that serve to give him a look of a little old dog, hence the name Albert.

His acceptance by my wider family was dented irrevocably after the incident of the shoe. We picked Albert up on 20th December 2007, but not as a Christmas dog; the timing was just coincidence. However, the problem of what to do with him over the festivities raised its head and so, as Lucy and I were going to different places, I volunteered to take him to my brother's for Christmas Eve. All went well until a faint but unmistakeable odour of a well-fed, non-house-trained pup broke across the dining table. Looking around for the source of the pong we finally alighted on my father-in-law's shoes, and there, in one of them, perfectly delivered were fresh puppy doings. My brother, after regaining some composure, instantly renamed his breed as a S**tShoe.

Poor old Kerwyn, who is now ten, did have a little bit of difficulty adapting to this horrendously bouncy and enthusiastic interloper. Even now, whilst he is very happy with the company, on odd occasions you can still see a pained expression synonymous with grumpy old men the world over; perhaps he should be renamed Victor.

As I write, Albert has been brought up to me, where he stands accused of removing eggshells from the bin and eating, or destroying them all over the carpet, but it's very hard to tell him off. Who would have a dog, eh?

GLENN HARROLD
AUTHOR

When asked to contribute to this book it was an easy one, as our dog Sable died last week and so this is a nice opportunity to tell her story. Ten years ago we found Sable in a local RSPCA rescue home. She was a lovely looking three-year-old lab cross but she had issues! She was literally bouncing off the walls in her kennel and when we got her home she went on a rampage. Within the first few weeks she bit my wife Aly, my mum, the postman and a few others. If I am totally honest I wanted to take this lunatic mutt back, but Aly insisted on keeping her in spite of the fact she was being attacked by Sable on a regular basis.

Aly set to work on Sable and much to my amusement began administering reiki, homeopathy, kinesiology and crystal healing on a daily basis. You name it, the dog had it; in fact she had more therapy treatments in a year than most people have in a lifetime! However, she began to respond to the treatment and love she received and quickly packed up biting people and started to show her real character. She soon turned into the most beautiful, loving pooch you could ever meet. Years later when we told her many admirers what a delinquent, nutty pooch she had once been people found it hard to believe! Mind you, my journey wasn't dissimilar – from drug-taking, delinquent punk rocker to best-selling self-help author! Me and the dog had a lot in common!

So there it is, a story with a happy ending. We had ten great years with her but one day last week, due to old age and failing health, she took a turn for the worse and we had no choice but to call the vet so she could be put to sleep. Before the vet came we had loads of visitors wanting to say goodbye to her, which was lovely. In the final hour, Aly and I held her and when the vet gave her the jab we said goodbye to our special canine companion.

Some dogs just have loads of character and intelligence and Sable had more than any dog I've ever known. We were heartbroken to lose her but comforted in the knowledge we gave her a fantastic life.

STEVEN HARTLEY
ACTOR

After the sad death of our first cat, Tybalt, my partner Abby and I decided that instead of opting for a kitten we would offer a home to a rescue cat.

We visited our local RSPCA rescue centre and saw a black and white moggy who seemed slightly eccentric but full of personality. Captain, as he had been named by the staff, had been mistreated and abandoned. He had arrived nervous, suffering from malnutrition and at around five years old had not yet been neutered.

At first glance he had very unique markings and a large 'tom cat' head. He also had the strange nervous habit of eating every time he was shown any kind of affection.

When we got him home he spent most of the first week behind the sofa with occasional forays around the kitchen and living room to eat and use the litter tray. After about a month indoors, Bisou, as Abby had now named him, was ready to go out. We quickly discovered he had never been outside in his life and his first few ventures were on the end of a long lead and spent spitting and hissing at the wind and any foreign smells.

After he had learned to use his cat flap he soon found his territory and is very protective. He cannot catch mice or birds - he is useless, but he will challenge any other animal in his realm. It is not unusual to see him squaring up to foxes and not unusual to have to take him to the vet with his wounds.

Bisou is the most vocal cat I have ever come across and will inform you of whatever he wants or is doing every hour. He is fantastic company, highly amusing and seems to be very grateful for the life he now has. He eats non-stop and puts on no weight, but I suspect as he gets older he will bear the facial scars of his 'tom cat' nature.

He is a wonderful addition to our family and I would urge anyone reading to save a rescue cat as it is so rewarding.

NIGEL HAVERS
ACTOR

My favourite pet is called Hottie - the smallest miniature smooth-haired Dachshund in the world. She belongs to my PA Jules, and is technically a witch as she has five toes on her front right paw. She has certainly bewitched me with her smile, bouncy gait and joi de vivre. I gave her a designer coat from Los Angeles recently - I forgot to buy my wife or daughter anything; I was too busy thinking of the grateful kisses I would get from Hottie.

STACEY HAYES
ACTRESS & MODEL

Growing up, my white Shepherd Elkie was my angel. As an adult, my cats Precious and Misha filled every day of my life for 15 years with joy. And now my cats Charlie Papa and Ebony bring me great happiness. I adore them, past and present. My life would be so empty and incomplete without the opportunity to love them.

AARON HESLEHURST
NEWS ANCHOR & PRESENTER

Oh how I loved this dog! Sir Lancelot - or just Lance, as we called him. This most magnificent Old English Sheepdog was my pet from the age of three to seventeen - and I spent many a day roaming around our property and the nearby bushland with him. Lance had the most striking eyes - one blue and one brown - and he was just such a loving dog. I will never forget how Lance used to leave our property's front gate and walk up to the main road to meet my sisters and me off the school bus every afternoon. Mum always knew when were due home, because Lance - how he knew this, I have no idea – would always head off to meet us about ten minutes before the bus was due. When we hopped off the bus Lance would always be there wagging his little stump of a tail and jumping in circles around us. Then we'd all walk home together.

Lance also loved a good swim! After all he was an Old English Sheepdog who endured the harsh Australian summers, but he had his ways of keeping cool - swimming with me in the pool was one of them. He'd just jump on in and we'd swim around together. Getting him out sometimes was a bit of a struggle!

Lance loved being around all of our other animals. We had show horses, which he loved running along with in the paddocks. He'd let our Cockatoo sit on his back. He'd play with the cats and, of course, in his later years he enjoyed the company of our other dog - a Dalmatian called Snoopy.

Over his fourteen-year life there are too many memories to list, but I will never forget his final day with us. Remarkably, Lance knew it was his time. He wandered off our property and walked with Snoopy for about a mile to a field - where he laid down and died! Snoopy just sat next to him and waited until we came and collected Lance. We buried him on our property - with a heavy heart and a lot of tears. He was a gift in my life and left a wonderful impression.

SCOTT HINDS
ACTOR

Common Name:	Senegal Parrot
Origin:	Africa
Life Span:	30 years
Size: Approx	9"
Habitat:	In the wild, Senegal Parrots eat fruits, seeds and grains. They are generally found in the edges where wooded areas meet Savannah or grassland areas.

Goose (our parrot) was found in someone's garden with wounds all over him, and he was named Goose after the character in the movie Top Gun, as he appeared to have crashed and burned. He had been rehomed three times either due to aggression or being too loud before he found a home with my wife and I. Vets were unable to tell us his age, as he doesn't have the typical markings of a young or old bird. He is a very friendly, loving bird who can be a little sensitive at times.

MICHELLE HORN
TELEVISION & RADIO PRESENTER

Dogs. I grew up in a home with dogs from the day I was born and have always been surrounded by them. I have fond and happy memories of them all - each with their individual character and their own funny ways. Of all the dogs we had at home, dear little Bonnie has always been my favourite. A tiny little thing, we bought her in Germany when my dad was based there. She was very dirty and smelly, so we took her home and cleaned her up. We were inseparable from day one. She was such a loving little thing and had such a cheeky character. She would delight in digging up all the newly planted flowers my dad had put in the garden. I'd be behind her attempting to replant them and sharing in my dad's bewilderment that all his plants were dying. I had a basket fitted to the front of my bike so that she could come with me when I went out. She was like royalty!

I now have a Parson Jack Russell called Rosie who is completely different, but crazy and fun. She spends her days swimming, running and rolling in anything unpleasant. She has been with us since she was two months old and is now eight years. She has taken the birth of our two kids in her stride and now loves having new and boisterous playmates.

I'll always have dogs - they are such loyal companions and are always excited to see you, even if you've just popped out the front door to go to the car! They are the best.

NORMAN HUDIS
TV & FILM SCRIPTWRITER

My favourite pet? Dusty. But this needs to be prefaced by the plain fact that I am not an animal lover. Good friends assured me, over the years, that one would come along and change all that. They were right.

He was a mixed Labrador and St Bernard, as big as a small pony. He was sheltering under my son Stephen's truck on the college parking lot, and when Steve shooed him out he promptly jumped into the passenger seat. Not having a crane handy, Steve had to leave him there and claim that the dog selected him ... Can we keep him, Dad? I'll look after him, etc.

His name had to be Dusty because that's what he was, after neglect for who knows how long. He appeared to sense the incredible – that old NH, immune to animals' charms, actually liked him and sat with that enormous head in my lap, pinning me to the couch of an evening.

But Dusty, for whatever remote and unknown reason, was incurably aggressive. He almost attacked the postman, a well-informed professional who, forgivingly, explained to me why dogs tend to go for these harmless public servants. It is, apparently, because the postman regularly approaches the house but is never invited in, therefore is unwelcome, a potential hostile intruder, and thus he attacks him as one who would do all inhabitants harm.

But it didn't stop there. Dusty went for all other animals. Once, when I was foolhardy enough to 'take him for a walk', we had hardly got out of the house when he spotted a small dog and took off at full pelt, in pursuit, wrenching the leash from my inexpert hand and bringing me to the ground.

There was nothing for it. 'Dad's dog' – an honoured and unique appellation - had to go to that 'big farm in the country' where the likes of Dusty could run free, harming no one and fulfilling their pounding energy. At least that's what parents, in such a fix, tell their kids. In fact, it was to the Pound, into which he trotted happily.

A month or so later, on the freeway I passed some kind of

truck and from out of the back window, I swear, Dusty peered, with every scrabbling sign of recognising and wanting to rejoin me. At least I hope it was him and that he was somehow on his way to someone who could cope with his, to me, frightening problems.

I thought for a while of writing 'Carry On Dusty' but, you know, for once I couldn't think of, or even invent, anything funny on those lines.

KIARA HUNTER
ACTRESS & SINGER (Canada)

My favourite pet has to be my twelve-year-old female Labrador Retriever named Dakota. She has been my best friend, roommate and exercise buddy since I got her when she was a four-month-old pup. I got her from a great breeder in South Dakota, USA, and she was shipped to me via plane to Vancouver, Canada.

When I got her she was the sweetest, most beautiful dog I have ever seen. Her loving nature and vivacious energy were infectious and we bonded immediately - an angel packaged in all black. I trained her immediately and she was easy. She can sit, stay, down, come, and there are many other commands that she excels at - as well, she is completely hand-trained whereby I don't use my voice at all. Dakota never growls or barks for no reason and definitely does not bite! She licks a lot though!

Dakota's favourite things to do are:
1. Chase: a ball, stick or anything that is throwable! She retrieves everything right back to your feet - so convenient!
2. Swim: I can't get her out of the water once she's in!
3. Eat: Labs are notorious for loving food and she's notorious for never saying 'no'!
4. Get Scratches: it's kind of embarrassing when she sticks her butt up in the air for a tail scratch, but people laugh so she's happy!
5. Talk: Dakota's communication skills are articulated with barks, whines, singing and grunting - very funny!
6. Be an Actress: she lets everyone know when she is pouting, happy, p****d off and excited - it's all in her eyes and body language.

I am blessed to have such a wonderful companion in my life. Dakota has brought me so much happiness, laughter, companionship and love - I will cherish all my moments with her for eternity.

Dakota, you are my love, my light and my angel. Thank you

for being you and for all the joy you have brought to me and everyone that you have touched. Let's continue to enjoy our relationship on this earth as it is a gift - and for that, I am thankful beyond words.

GEOFFREY HUTCHINGS
ACTOR

I know this is supposed to be about a favourite pet, but this is about my most hated pet - the most boring creature on God's earth!

If you have children, at some time in your life you've probably had to suffer it. Large jar? Remember? Lots of leaves? ... And the STICK INSECT!

Very aptly named. Not because it resembles a stick. No. But because that's all it does. It doesn't go anywhere. It doesn't do anything. It just sticks. A ginger-beer plant is more exciting.

And they multiply at a rate faster than rabbits! One minute there are a few and the next minute thousands. How they achieve coition is a complete mystery to me. It must be fraught with danger. As every backwoodsman knows, two stick insects rubbing against each other – instant conflagration. Bear Grylls has been using them for years.

Why isn't there some really macho version? Like a log insect? One that you could take for walks – on a lead? Oh, yes, of course there is! A crocodile!

JOHN INVERDALE
SPORTS PRESENTER

One of my favourite pets is a goldfish called Motivator. I won him at the Derby fair on Epsom Downs the year Motivator won the great race, and so he was suitably christened. Every subsequent year a goldfish has been won and has been duly named after that year's winner, but none has made it beyond the Prix de L'Arc de Triomphe later that summer – that is, except for Motivator, who keeps on swimming round and round, taking on and outliving all-comers. Just how long can goldfish live? How many miles has he swum in all that time? I've just checked on him and he's still there - apparently happy enough. A very soothing and reliable presence in the corner of the room.

DEBORAH JEFFREY
ACTRESS

Sandy was an inappropriately named tri-colour Cocker Spaniel. She was the sweetest, most charming, daftest, most entertaining little softy, who was very partial to my then boyfriend's (now husband) leg - she tried to love him intensely, but there was only one girl for him!

As she got older, she got smellier, randier and even more short-sighted and had extremely selective hearing. In these latter years she would shrug you off if you called her, blatantly using her 'deafness' to her advantage, while she sniffed and snuffled a while longer in the hope you didn't notice she was taking more time than usual. However, she was caught out one evening, and this story remains to be one of my favourite anecdotes about her to this day.

Imagine a 14-year old Cocker, curled up in her bed in the living room, cosily sleeping to the hum of the TV and the low murmur of conversation from my dad and my little brother as they interacted with the programme they were watching; her scruff and ears and other fluff and loose skin, quite popular with Spaniels, falling (or at her age drooping) over her face, scrunched up in her reverie.

Then - the sudden, startled, intense, alert, shocked, rude awakening she experienced flashing across her face, to her haunches, her screwed-up eyes trying to open quickly but a little dazzled from the light, her floppy ears now arched and stiff! Why? Because my dad had let off the loudest, most almighty bottom rip to make even the BFG proud! Her movement was so sudden and so staccato that my dad and brother chain-reacted to her in a shock to rival hers - yet, once realisation hit half a second later, their laughter ensured that they told the tale to family and friends that knew Sandy! Just the utter description - of knowing she had cataracts and couldn't see, was hard of hearing, was old and rickety - then, suddenly, in your mind's eye try to picture her in fright/flight/fight mode - it's hilarious - as if she could have used her adrenalin usefully! Bless her faux-cotton socks.

ELENA JUATCO
SINGER & ACTRESS (Canada)

I think I could talk forever about my dog. It's like asking parents about their kids, or grandparents about their grandchildren, or kids who go to camp about camp, or Politics majors about the war, or Economist majors about debits and credits, Quebeckers about separating from Canada or where the best poutine joint is, Filipinos about rice, 20-year-olds about their experiences backpacking through Europe, actors about bad acting or their upcoming fringe show, poets about the colour of the sunset, Canucks fans about Leafs fans, Leafs fans about Habs fans, Vancouverites about good weed, Maritimers about good seafood, police officers about firemen, firemen about who's making dinner, Grandpa about what it was like growing up ... you get the point? She's my favourite thing to talk about.

I think it is because I wanted a dog for as long as I can remember. My brother and I constantly harassed my parents about the idea when we were growing up. They instead tried to fill the void with stuffed animals and virtual Tamagotchis. Needless to say, it just wasn't the same thing! After Goldy, Whitey, Sharky and Sushi were all flushed into the ocean, I had absolutely no desire for another fish and was tired of feigning interest in aquatic life and electronic pets. The charade was up. I was not willing to settle any more. I wanted a DOG. A beautiful, big, loving friend that I could hug and talk to, knowing that she was listening to me and cared.

Then that wondrous day came!

Our house got broken into ...

My mother sat, distraught, on the couch as my father slowly paced back and forth in the next room. My brother and I sat silently on the ottoman, expecting someone to start yelling. Then my father stormed into the living room, walking heavily and with purpose. With his right hand perched on hip and his left hand pointing high into the air, he declared, "KIDS! WE ARE GETTING A DOG!"

"Yaaayyyy!" my brother and I exclaimed with subtle and

51

restrained enthusiasm so as not to press our luck.

"Larrrrreee …," my mother cautioned. But she was outnumbered.

Thus began the search for Cola. My dad wanted the scariest, meanest, most indestructible-looking dog and immediately researched Rottweilers. My mother, always the practical one, leaned away from dogs who had 'kill' or 'attack' as possible words in their vocabulary. She began researching protection dogs. "We need a dog with a good bark," she would say.

A family friend recommended the Bouvier des Flandres, a wonderful protection dog with a calm temperament and a good, solid bark. And they were pretty darn cute too. SOLD! We watched The Dog of Flanders in preparation for our new life with our dog. My mother purchased every 'How to train a dog' book available. She soon realised that she was doing more research on getting a dog than she did before having kids. It was a big undertaking.

Cola arrived one wonderful fall evening, crawling out of her little cage and immediately peeing on the carpet. A great start!

She was a dream! She was perfect! While my mother was constantly wary of her having accidents around the house, she rarely did (though I probably thought that because it was never me that had to clean them up). She just was! She would sit there, looking at you; wonder about what you were saying to her, trying to make sense of your human words.

I remember the day before her neutering appointment. My dad shook his finger at her and said, "Ohhh! You are going to GET it! You are gonna REALLY get it!" She looked at him with confused but curious eyes.

What is going on? Why is he talking to me like that? Why are Leonard and Elena dancing around the living room? Is something wrong? An intruder? Must bark. Woof! Who are all these little kids running around the living room this fine Christmas evening? Where did they come from? Where did all these people come from? Must herd! Must herd little children together so as not to lose track of one. Who is that person in our backyard with the yellow rain jacket? INTRUDER! Must bark! WOOF WOOF WOOF! Oh - it's Daddy! That was stupid. But still must bark – WOOF WOOF! What is that noise? In the distance … an ambulance? Trouble? Danger? This calls for Cola Bear. Must bark - WOOF WOOF! Siren getting louder! Must howl – AWWOOOOOO!

I often wonder as to what exactly goes through Cola's head when she looks at me with her big brown eyes when I talk to her. She's a very involved listener and sometimes she'll open her mouth as if she has a response but can't get the words out. When I tell her I'll walk her later in the day, she remembers. So when I don't, she gives me the most bitter glare. My dad would call from upstairs, "Elena! Were you going to walk the dog?" "AWWWOOOO!" she would interject. I just can't say no to this dog!

After I got my painful wisdom teeth removed, she moaned with me and slept beside me on the couch as I was knocked out on painkillers. Cola has a sixth sense about our family's well-being, and if on any day you are feeling under the weather she will follow you around the house and try to keep you safe. When she sees my big red luggage bag coming down the stairs she knows that I'm leaving to go away, so she'll start whining and following me around the house. Elena's leaving AGAIN. No, no, no ... why? Was it something I did?

But she always remembers me every time I come back home and we just pick up from where we left off. Every time I come through that front door she gets so excited. She can hardly believe I'm actually home. I knew you'd come back! You're back! Though sometimes when I return home she refrains from jumping up and down excitedly and instead she calmly approaches me to get petted. People will say, "Maybe she forgot you," but that is beyond impossible. She's just being bitter with me. You keep LEAVING. Why do you keep LEAVING? Am I not good enough for you anymore? I can't take this anymore. You being away, it's too much ...

It's the hardest part of my job – leaving home all the time. I wish she could travel the country with me. Sometimes I wish it just as much as I wish she could go take herself on a walk and bag her own poo and put it in the trash herself along with her other excrement. But Cola, you are so worth the poop scooping and the stinky fur and the hourly periods of barking at the gardener when I'm trying to catch up on sleep. You are my best friend. I've been waiting my whole life for you.

JASON KARL
TELEVISION PRESENTER

Animals have always played an important role in my life, and pets have been very much part of my family from a very young age.

My first cat was a farmhouse kitten, born at the foot of mysterious Pendle Hill in Lancashire - haunt of the Pendle witches. Friends of my parents were kind enough to let us take home a small tabby handful following a visit one day, and back in Surrey, Pendle, as we named him, quickly shrugged off his rural background and made a name for himself at our family home, later moving with us to Oxfordshire.

My second cat was Merlin, the 'ghost-hunting cat'; not really my cat at all, but rather a cat who chose me to look after him! While living in an old house built in the eleventh century, Merlin graced the flagstoned floors with his presence, reclining for a little petting when it suited him and sleeping on my bed each night, guarding me from the unseen 'ghosts' reputed to haunt the house.

Less inclined to hunt ghosts were Gobbolino and Casper, two felines rescued by myself and my partner from the Cats Rescue charity. I remember visiting a home filled with literally dozens of cats needing good homes.

Casper was quickly chosen, and I spotted Gobbolino sitting quietly on a shelf in the corner while all around him were scurrying and demanding attention. I picked him as a new 'brother' for Casper and, after sitting nervously in the cup of my hand, a few strokes later he was purring! I decided on the name Gobbolino after remembering a story from my childhood named Gobbolino, the Witch's Cat, by Ursula Moray Williams. Later, after Casper had passed on, Gobbolino was joined by a female cat, Sootica - or Soots for short.

When I moved into a large Victorian town house I decided there was enough space for a few more feline friends, and in came Pagan and Aslan; another two rescue cats, this time from the RSPCA. Living a few doors down from a Baptist church, I wanted an excuse to shout "Pagan" at the top of my voice down the road, a mischievous joke that has amused many over the years!

I now live with four cats - Sootica, Pagan, Aslan and Pumpkin - a ginger stray whom I found wandering the streets in 2001. Barely a month old, he was in great distress when I found him, and after bundling him up and taking him home he slept for half a day on our sofa before waking to meet his new cat family - as the youngest he is the most boisterous and keeps the others in line!

ARDEN KAYCE
ACTRESS & PRODUCER (US)

Hummingbirds are my favourite creatures because they symbolise all things beautiful! They're magical, inspirational and are a constant reminder of God's gift of life. The essence of their beauty reminds me to live life to the fullest!

IAN KELLY
ACTOR, WRITER & TELEVISION PRESENTER

Dylan the dog is well known in publishing and acting, as I take
him everywhere. A preternaturally well-behaved, accidental
star, therefore, of screen and stage ... but a disaster on radio -
too quiet. Also a regular fixture at Hatchards' Authors of the
Year parties, etc.

KATHERINE KELLY
ACTRESS

I have always loved animals, especially cats, dogs and budgies. Over the years we have had an assortment of all these, but at present I just have my lovely cat, who is named after Indiana Jones as he is extremely adventurous.

He climbs up the chimney when visiting my parents, so at Christmas we had our very own Santa CLAWS; he also climbed the Christmas tree, bringing it down on top of him. I have attached a photograph of him enjoying the wrapping of our presents amongst the debris.

MATTHEW KELLY
ACTOR & TELEVISION PRESENTER

I have only owned one pet (or did she own me?). An amazing Old English Sheepdog, called Cassie, found me years ago and decided to adopt me.

She was an absolute lady, gentle and wise, and phased by nothing. Although frightened and unsure when she first came to live with me, she soon had me exactly where she wanted me. She came with me nearly everywhere and was equally at home in theatre green rooms and TV studios, taking my chaotic lifestyle in her stride – everyone who met her, adored her.

As she grew older she developed a heart condition and was given only a couple of months to live. This was not acceptable to Cassie, who lived a full and loving life for another two years!

She and I shared something quite extraordinary: an unconditional and total love. I still miss her but am always thankful that she decided to share her life with me.

ROSS KING
TELEVISION PRESENTER

My pet! What a pet, what a weekend, what a way to lose the pet and your friends too!

Mum and Dad said, "Yes, of course you can have the school pet hamster, Hammy, home for the weekend. It'll also let us see how responsible you are ... maybe we'll get you one of your own."

Friday:
4.45. Home from school with the class favourite.
4.55. Wouldn't it be great to let the little fella out the cage ... DOH! Straight into the kitchen, behind the cupboards, couldn't be found until Sunday night. He came out unhurt but hungry ... Yippee!

Monday morning:
Panic over, Hammy's in his cage ... Run to the car, Dad's waiting ... And, yes - I trip, cage falls, door opens ... Hammy is free - forever.

Hammy, if you read this please come back ... I promise I'll take good care of you this time!

Ally Begg
CASPER

Julia Bradbury
LOTTE

Geoff Capes
ONE OF HIS BUDGIES

Sheila Collins
MISTY AND TANSY

Venda D'Abato
MAX

Anna Easteden
HER DOG

Marcus Harris
KERWYN

Marcus Harris
ALBERT

Steven Hartley
BISOU

Stacey Hayes
CHARLIE PAPA

Kiara Hunter
DAKOTA

Deborah Jeffrey
SANDY

Elana Juatco
COLA

Jason Karl
PUMPKIN

Jason Karl
PAGAN & ASLAN

Ian Kelly
DYLAN

Bonnie-Jill Laflin
ONE OF HER DOGS

Suzi Lorraine
LOKI AND MONKI

Linda Lusardi
KOKO

Beth Maitland
DRAAKHART

Skye McCole Bartusiak
PIPPA AND BEVO

Michael McKell
GREMLIN

Emma Milne
PAN & BADGER

Radha Nillia and Ayvee Verzonilla
BELLA AND JAH KING

Chris Packham
'MAD MATES'

Alisa Reyes
BOOTSY

Hayley Tamaddon
OZZY

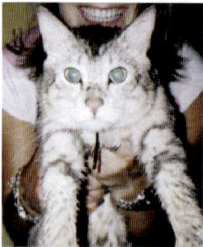

Jane Tonks
TEDDY

Dawn Walters
PCHŁA

Lucy Williamson
DAISY-BOO

Xixi Yang
TREKKIE

BONNIE-JILL LAFLIN
ACTRESS & MODEL (US)

My three rescues, Diamond Chanel, Wilt Chamberlain and Norma Jean, are my world!

They always know how to make me smile when I'm down. The companionship and warmth they bring me every day are something I feel so lucky to have in my life. I couldn't be happier to give such amazing animals a safe and loving home.

BRIDIE LATONA
ACTRESS

This is my dog Brutus. He loves the snow, loves rolling in it and getting covered in it. I love the lifelong loyalty of dogs. Brutus never fails to greet me with enthusiasm and a wagging tail. He only ever sees the good side of you. I love the way Brutus comes and puts his head gently on my lap and looks up at me with those soulful eyes. Sometimes he drags his bed over to the dinner table or wherever we are sitting just to be close.

We saved Brutus from the pound when he was a tiny puppy. He had been found dumped by a river with his brothers and sisters. I think it adds a special meaning to get a dog from the pound. It feels great to be able to give them a good life that they might not have had, to give them all the love and attention that they deserve. They appreciate every moment.

HELEN LEDERER
ACTRESS

When my daughter was five I asked around for a kitten. Dawn French suggested Daisy (née Merry) who was a kitten belonging to Emma Freud and Richard Curtis. Such a very well connected cat! Daisy had no tail and scratched my daughter, but Hannah chose her – over her brothers with tails. Everyone always asked us what we did with her tail!

Daisy was kind and cuddly and Hannah trained her well. She loved people and everyone commented on her. She was not afraid of anyone and would turn up to cuddle if she felt we were sad. We miss her SO much. She was a 'one-off' and we were blessed to have her. Daisy leaves three offspring cats – two boys and a girl - who are loved up by a friend in Brighton.

IAIN LEE
TELEVISION PRESENTER & COMEDIAN

My favourite pet is my lazy black cat called Velvet. I got her about eight years ago from a pub that was getting rid of her because she was being bullied by another cat there, Guinness.

When I got her I was told she was a quiet, timid little thing that barely squeaked, hardly sat on laps and certainly wouldn't want to go out. For a while, that was true. She spent the first six weeks hiding behind the sofa, only venturing out when I had gone to bed. After a few weeks, I would sometimes glance down and see her sat beside me, only to see her shoot off again, knowing she'd been rumbled.

Now, this ten-year-old lady is a cocky little so and so. She is the boss and gets what she wants. Her most endearing quality is she comes and gets me and my wife when she thinks it's bedtime. At around 10 p.m., she comes into the living room and starts getting in everyone's way – jumping on and off the sofa, sitting so we can't see the TV and generally being a nuisance. Anytime one of us stands up, she starts heading towards the bedroom as if to say, "Come on, you lot, I'm tired, it's bedtime"!

She also doesn't like waiting for breakfast and used to wake us up every morning at 5 a.m. to be fed. She would do this by first jumping around the bed, then knocking stuff off the bedside tables, and if that didn't work she would sit on my wife's chest and start tapping her face. She now gets her breakfast from an automatic feeder, allowing us to sleep a little longer.

She's not a great mouser - I have seen her just batting one back and forth - but she did go through a thing of bringing us gifts. I once caught her coming in through the cat flap looking very guilty. When I asked her what she was up to she slowly lowered her head to the floor and opened her mouth to allow a baby frog to hop out. I spent the next 20 minutes trying to catch the bloody thing in a saucepan.

Velvet is great company, knows when I'm depressed or sad, and always comes along at just the right moment to cheer you up. As I type this, she is sat behind me on the sofa, fast asleep, looking adorable. The best cat in the world.

VALERIE LEON
ACTRESS

When my children were young we had a ginger tom cat called Jim, and whenever I was late home he would be waiting at the top of our road having heard my car engine, and when I had parked he would trot in front of me till we got to my front door. I found this very sweet.

Also before that we had a dog that was a cross between a Bull Mastiff and a Dalmatian. My husband asked me to take him on trial; he'd met a man in Barclays bank who said he had to have the dog destroyed as he lived in a flat and couldn't keep him. Although not a dog lover I took him in, and when I was pregnant with my first child, despite his size, he would nuzzle at me gently!

STEVE LEONARD
VETERINARY SURGEON & WILDLIFE PRESENTER

Useless and her two sisters (Juicy and Huge) were orphaned at only a couple of weeks. They arrived at the veterinary practice at the same time as I did, freshly qualified from university and ready to work (me, not the kittens).

The nurses took barely four weeks to persuade me to bring all three kittens home to my little end terrace where they proved to be far more entertaining than television, ambushing each other and failing to quite make the leap between the sofas.

Unfortunately I lost both of Useless's sisters on the roads over the next couple of years, which was heartbreaking. Ten years on and Useless is still the reassuring weight on the end of my bed that lets me know I'm home. She is constantly on a diet, as she loves her food just too much, is on twice daily injections for diabetes and has anti-inflammatories for arthritis. She drools with contentment when given any fuss and sheds enough hair for ten cats. She's perfect.

RAY LEWIS
FORMER FOOTBALL (PREMIER LEAGUE) REFEREE

We have always had Cocker Spaniels.

The first one we had, 40 years ago, was a golden Cocker named Lewis (highly original!) The second was a black and white Spaniel named Snoopy and the third was a black Spaniel named Daisy. Lastly came Demma, who is golden and was 13 a couple of weeks ago.

They have all been lovely in their different ways. I know you shouldn't have favourites, but I am very close to Demma.

SUZI LORRAINE
ACTRESS & MODEL (US)

No matter what kind of day I've had, there's nothing better than opening the front door and being greeted by my two little devil cats. Loki and Monki are two wily black cats that I adopted from an animal shelter. I am an animal rights activist and firmly believe that animals should be adopted from shelters - not breeders. There are so many homeless animals in this world. The numbers are staggering! Many of these shelter cats and dogs are euthanised due to lack of room in the shelters, while puppy mills and breeders keep popping out new pure breds. Please, everyone - adopt from shelters, and make sure you get your animal spayed.

I named Loki, aptly, after the Norse God of Mischief. My mother always told me: be careful - animals will live up to their names for better or worse. Loki was a 'Loki' from day one. He's the sweetest and most affectionate cat you could hope to meet. He has a touch of Oriental Short Hair in him, so his features are a bit odd and exotic. He has big ears, an elongated nose, and a very angular-shaped face. He is also a little devil. One of his best 'tricks' included crawling beneath my bed, strategically pulling down the material on the underside of the mattress, and building a hammock that he could lounge in.

Loki can't deal with closed doors, and if locked out of the bedroom will stand there and cry, scream and caterwaul for five hours. It's louder than having a baby. He must always be in the middle of things. He's thin and sleek, but he has always had these huge claws/paws. During a visit to the vet when he was just a baby kitten, he was dutifully resting in his carrier, waiting to get the visit over with. All of a sudden, he reached through the holes in the top of the carrier, extended his arm all the way through, and outstretched his claws like Freddy Krueger. He then retracted and pulled back into the cage. A woman sitting nearby with a little poodle said, "What kind of animal IS that?" I think she thought he was a baby puma!

Monki came along a short while later. Again, he had no problem living up to his name. My Monki's favourite 'trick' is jumping on my pillow while I'm sleeping, and nesting for ten minutes in my hair before settling in. He claws and paws at my hair until he has achieved the exact 'style' he's looking for - usually somewhere between Don King and Amy Winehouse. Monki is as round as Loki is lean, with a jovial little baby face and a portly belly. Monki also has a beautiful singing voice. If you pick him up and hold him a certain way, he seriously sings! It sounds like a cross between a baby Pavarotti and those ghosts that people display during Halloween. "Whoooo ... ahhhhhh ... ooooooh ...." He has this fantastic vibrato and a multi-octave range. You must see it ... er, hear it ... to believe it! He is also a bit of a klepto. At a recent house-warming party he strolled right up to a guest's dinner plate and made off like a bandit with a piece of food. He returned to said plate later and began lapping up creamed spinach with reckless abandon. Yes, creamed spinach! Since the incident, we have been working on manners ...

NORMAN LOVETT
ACTOR & COMEDIAN

When I was a little boy of around nine or ten I had a pet rabbit called Snowy. A buck or a doe, I really don't know. One day I let Snowy out of his/her hutch and we played in the garden, but after a few minutes Snowy suddenly ran off hotly pursued by a cat. I could only stand and watch as the pair of them speeded towards a load of bushes at the bottom of my garden. Then the most incredible thing happened - as Snowy got to the bushes he suddenly did a U-turn and ran back towards me, stopping at my feet and panting heavily. I gratefully picked Snowy up and put him/her back into the hutch. I remember that incident as if it were yesterday.

LINDA LUSARDI
MODEL & ACTRESS

My dog Koko. I would have loved another baby but age wasn't on my side, so I bought a minute Dachshund instead. We called her Koko and she is the sweetest little dog I have ever encountered. She has the cuddliest soft coat I have ever felt. We have had her for four years and my daughter Lucy, 12, and my son Jack, 9, love her as much as I do. She completes our family and she keeps me company when my husband Sam is on tour. She snuggles next to me on the couch while I watch TV and she sleeps with me when I'm on my own. She puts up with so much, especially when the children were younger, and she only barks when someone comes to the door. I was never allowed a dog as a child and now our house would seem empty without her. I didn't realise you could love an animal so much. She really is my third baby..

BETH MAITLAND
ACTRESS (US)

I have a long and complicated love of animals...but I had to wait till I was 16 to get a real pet of my own. This was the dainty Sheltie, Noelle, who I loved, but had to leave at home when I moved off to Hollywood to pursue my dreams. When I finally was cast in a regular job, I went straight out and got my darling Spenser (named for the poet), a blue merle Australian Shepherd. Then came Guido the stray black cat, then I added Rosie, my first horse, an Appaloosa mare...followed by Shoshone, the Strawberry Roan gelding who was crossed with a Belgian draft horse, and was a big red beauty. Then there was little Matilda, another blue Merle Aussie...she was with me only briefly, but I rescued her from a terrible fate, and I miss her every day. And more cats, Reggie the Tuxedo cat, Titania and Oberon, the pair of stray kittens, and Buffie, the blonde tiger cat from the pound.

I adopted Beanie, the Airedale terrier. She once saved my toddler daughter from a snake attack and took several bites on the nose before killing the serpent and saving the fair maiden - what a devoted and single minded dog!! She ate $1200 worth of shoes...only one of each pair, of course, in her anxiety when I had to leave the house, so I got her a friend, the gentle and beautiful Border Collie/Akita mix, Lily, who had the most tender spirit, and comforted me by leaning on me each time she saw me cry. Then I married...and things got more complicated! My husband had Weimeraners, Ziggy and the young twin sisters, Gertrude and Hildegarde. So we had to buy a ranch big enough to hold our growing brood. My husband had Dallas, the quarter horse gelding. I now had a gorgeous running quarter buckskin mare, Maza (and her two daughters, Goldie and Fling) We added various breeds of chickens (sharing eggs with our friends in three colours), three lovely little goats (Pansy, Petunia, and Periwinkle Rose) the latter of which is an angora, so I learned to spin her snowy hair. Then came my beloved Shakespeare, another blue merle Aussie and later another Weimeraner, Leibchen. We rescued a Parson's Jack Russell for my daughter - he's still with us - called Tuffy McDuff, and we also rescued a wire haired Fox Terrier, Sprocket. He systematically dismantles everything he finds: lawn sprinklers, tennis balls, plastic containers, and pet beds! When Shakespeare left us, I decided to change breeds. I got a Bouvier de Flanders dog, Hercule Poirot, or Hairy for short. I trained him in French after his Belgian namesake, confounding the groomer, until he settled into our bi-lingual household and learned English too! Hairy has become my darling companion in chores, canyon walks and evenings watching the sunset. He is much more protective than any dog I've had before - it takes some time before he stops protecting me and lets people into our home - but what a beautiful and gentle giant he is, and is wonderful with the other dogs. So our dog family includes Leibchen, the two terriers and Hairy – a motley canine crew. We have just a handful of chickens now and are down to two little blonde goats, entertaining and eager to keep the weeds down and finish the table scraps and garden cuttings. The horses include the aged Maza, now 32 years old, her 20 year old daughter, Fling, and a new buckskin colt for my daughter, named Dakota Doug. And now, my favourite of all! Two years ago, I bought my Friesian Ster gelding, Draakhart, with whom I do dressage. I have never known a horse like him - he is more a like a dog and follows me everywhere. I save peppermint candies for him in my car so he's learned to run to it and poke his head in the window for his sweet! I wish everyone was as happy to see me as he is! He will do anything for a cookie, so has learned loads of tricks. I hung a cowbell in a tree and he's learned to "ring the bell for mama." I'm pragmatic enough to know it's really for the cookie! He is affectionate, majestic, knightly, glorious. And would jump through fire for me. He and my Bouvier are my favourites for now, but I have to say, that I am certain there will be more favourites to come. The love, devotion and companionship received from the pets I've loved, and those yet to come to me, are things I could not live without. I have a like-minded, animal loving friend who swears, "you can grieve for a lost pet better while throwing a ball to your new puppy." And truer words were never spoken. So many of my loving furry friends needed to be rescued, but no one needed them more than I. I am honoured to have loved so many animals, and look forward to loving many more. We are stewards of these devoted pets - there is no greater reward than a wagging tail or eager lick - **thank goodness for them all!**

RODNEY MARSH
FORMER PROFESSIONAL FOOTBALLER

Over the years, dogs have always been a huge part of the Marsh family.

All girls, they started with Chelsea, who was a rescue dog (yellow Lab). Due to bad hips and lots of ailments, we lost her at the very young age of 8 months old, which upset the whole family terribly. Immediately after, we decided to get Stepney, the first Golden Retriever, a beautiful dog, and it wasn't too long before we got a little mate for her, another Golden called Putney, who had the most wonderful disposition of all. Putney and Stepney were so close and did everything together, which made it easy when the Marsh family travelled from time to time.

Stepney passed away aged twelve and a half, followed by Putney, who lived to twelve. Her death upset the family more than any other. She died of cancer one morning when she was laying under the breakfast table and her organs gave out. We were all crying for weeks and it took a very long time to get over her loss.

My son Jonathan, trying to alleviate the heartache of Putney's death, brought home Rosie (yet another Golden), aged five weeks - a mistake to take her from her mother so young. It's fair to say that Rosie was the devil dog. Having no maternal discipline and being the alpha influence, she was uncontrollable, but she still brought us much joy and happiness and was tied to my wife Jean's hip - every time Jean left the room, Rosie would follow. Rosie unfortunately died in January this year at age eight. Currently the Marsh family is 'dogless' after twenty-five years of having at least one dog under our roof, but that may change very soon!

It's safe to say that our dogs have been a big part of our life and have brought us so much joy!

JAMES MAW
BROADCASTER & WRITER

'Miss Pip'. If you ever visited the silver-screen star Greta Garbo in her dotage then you will have some idea what it's like to visit Miss Pip now that she is 93, in cat years. With her great lion's mane of a ruff and her tail flailing around in the air, she is still rather grand, but then she came from a theatrical family - both her parents were in shows. Sitting by the hearth, she will still hold you with those steely blue eyes, staring out between chocolate ears, waiting for her close-up. You immediately know that you are in the presence of a very great actress when you meet Miss Pip. Like many a dame of stage and screen she has her peculiarities. Like Garbo she can be reclusive, especially if an empty cardboard box is brought into the house, and just as Greta Garbo herself was said to do, Miss Pip steals lamb chops, and she carries them in her mouth into the bathroom and hides them in slippers! She still has her funny little ways, but then Miss Pip was a TV star known to millions in her day. She is allowed her foibles; and her fur-balls. At 93 she no longer performs on screen - she is resting, as they say in the business, mostly by the radiator. What a career she has had!

On the day when we set off to the Granada TV studios in Manchester for her audition to become the new Coronation Street cat, we were full of hope, but the producer of this gritty northern soap just could not see what she would bring to the part. He could not imagine how a white and chocolate, extremely fluffy pedigree Birman would fit in with the dour brick and drizzle of that famous street, waving her fluffy tail imperiously as she wandered along the railway viaduct. It was a blow. There are only a few gaps in the market for cats in television. Undeterred, her big break finally came one Saturday afternoon when she was called in to the studios for a part in the Granada sitcom Watching. She had been cast in the role of Spinoza, a part almost written for her. Even Shakespeare hadn't written a good part for a cat, though he did write one for a bear. I had no idea how Miss Pip had secured the role until I learned that she had slept with the director! She often came to work with me and she had curled up on his desk for an entire afternoon. Dorothy, his assistant, rang me. "Would you bring Miss Pip in for a rehearsal?" "You want her to rehearse?" I said. "You want a cat to rehearse?" "It's a full dress-run," said Dorothy. "And that means ALL the cast." "Miss Pip does not rehearse," I said. "She feels that a dog might practise its hoop-jumping tricks; a dolphin may train for water shows, but a Birman does not rehearse. A Birman is always quite perfect first time." "But in this episode Malcolm leaves home," Dorothy explained. "And she has to jump into his suitcase and go with him." "Don't worry, Dorothy," I assured her. "Miss Pip always jumps into suitcases. She just can't resist it." On the night of the recording of the show I watched nervously with a stagehand as Miss Pip was led on set in front of the audience. As the cameras were about to roll I turned to the stagehand and asked if anyone had thought to put peeled prawns in the suitcase to encourage her jump into it. "Oh blimey," he said "It's just shirts and socks." The tape began running and lights flooded the set. The actor entered the set of his bedroom, threw open his suitcase, lying on the bed, and left the room. All cameras focused on Miss Pip, sitting on the end of the bed. Casually she looked at the door. Then she looked at the suitcase. She turned to gaze at where there was a window – and then jumped into the suitcase! The audience cheered. The director declared it a take-in-one. The cat was in the suitcase! It was her greatest triumph. The stagehand grabbed me by the arm. "That's some cat," he said. "That's Miss Pip," I replied. "She's a professional." "She must have read the script," he said, shaking his head. "Of course she did," I said. "It's been lining her litter tray for a week!" Stunned by Miss Pip's obvious natural ability, she was engaged for a further three series then and there! That night they hung a star on her cat basket. From then on she shared a dressing room with Liza Tarbuck.

With fame and public acclaim came many demands on her time, endless travel, endless meetings and charity work, and her life began to follow a course much like that of Angelina Jolie.

Then in the early nineties she disappeared from public view. She went missing shortly after moving to a new apartment. Miss Pip left no clues behind her except an open window flapping in the breeze. She hadn't taken anything with her, not her diamanté collar, or even a lamb chop. As the hours and days went by, a major cat hunt was launched by her friends and fans, but no trace of her could be found. Had her sudden fame been too much to bear? Had a fellow actress ruffled her fur? Had her exhaustive work schedule of half an hour a week become too much; or worse, had she been kidnapped for a ransom? We scoured the banks of the Manchester Ship Canal but came up with nothing but shopping trolleys. We alerted the Manchester Evening News, but there was no sign of her, not even a fur-ball could be found. Then on the sixth day the Editor of the Manchester Evening News unravelled the mystery. She had been on the roof! Miss Pip had found her way through the skylight of an empty penthouse apartment next door, the one sole location that had not been searched, and there she had been for five long days. "Like Garbo," said the Editor, "she just wanted to be alone." It was peeled prawns for tea that night!

Miss Pip's life, however, was to be overturned again. She had just signed to work with one of television's greats, Jeremy Beadle, in You've Been Framed! – or 'You've Been Scratched!' as we called it. While professionally her star was at its apogee, privately there was upheaval; there was no longer a part for her in my life. Increasingly reporting from abroad, I knew that her talents were unsuited to reporting from war zones and that it may have looked a little odd if, as the Molotov cocktails flew over, I reported with a white fluffy cat on a blue suede leash. So I left for Cambodia and she left for a post at Manchester University - a scratching post! She moved in with Robin Marshall, Professor of Physics, and there she lives happily to this day. At the tail end of her career she lives the life of a Cheshire Cat, sitting for hours in the window, pursuing her great interest in ornithology.

I visit her often and I can confirm: Miss Pip still jumps in suitcases, reliving her famous scene ....

KIRSTY McCABE
TELEVISION PRESENTER

Around seven years ago a small ginger cat kept visiting me at my flat in south London. I started feeding said cat and when it was ill I took it to the vet. In return, he purred extremely loudly, slept during the day with me if I was on night shifts, and mopped up the tears when my heart was broken. After four years I figured we were a team, so when I moved Ginger came too. But just in case he still had his original owner, I asked my old neighbours to look out for any missing cat posters. To our great relief (mine and Ginger's), none appeared.

These days he's not so small; in fact he's on a diet! But that hasn't stopped him making friends in his new neighbourhood. He likes to roam the streets with his doppelgänger, a slightly more streamlined ginger tom. And his favourite companion is our neighbour's cat Misty; they will stand outside each other's cat flaps meowing at whoever is lazing around inside (usually Ginger) to come and play.

Sometimes I wonder if Ginger is a dog trapped in a cat's body. He comes when you whistle, he loves to be cuddled and he likes to go for walks with me. I couldn't ask for more, although it would be nice if he'd stop leaping onto my head in the middle of the night when I'm sleeping and he's hungry .....

SKYE McCOLE BARTUSIAK
ACTRESS (US)

My favourite dogs are Maltese. I have two favourites I take to all film sets. Pippa is my ten-year-old female who is paralysed on one side of her body and lost an eye from a tragic car accident. She is high maintenance because of her high needs, but I love nurturing her. She needs a liquid diet and I carry her almost everywhere as it is hard for her to get around, and because of her paralysis it is difficult for her to eat so she needs nutritional attention. I named her Pippa after my first major film role when I was five! That was my name in Stephen King's Storm of the Century. I also have a male dog, Bevo, that I named after the University of Texas mascot ... Go Longhorns! He is six months old and I think he needs a visit from the Dog Whisperer! I think he will be a senior citizen before I get him housebroken or, for that matter, leash broken! No matter what, they are solid family members and I cannot imagine not having pets to love.

MICHAEL McKELL
ACTOR

Gremlin. In 1990 my then partner, Diane, had been offered a puppy. Each night Diane would say the same things: "Can we have the puppy? His father was a champion. I'll take it to work with me. It will be no trouble." One cold winter's Sunday morning I cracked. "Okay, where are we going?" She smiled, "Wales."

We pulled into a snowy track that led to a York stone farmhouse. There were many outbuildings and the usual suspects of chickens, a lone sheep and a very exotic looking long-haired black cat who stared knowingly at me - "sucker". After a brief meeting with the manager, Diane left me drinking sweet tea whilst she went to one of the outbuildings to pick up our gift! She returned cradling in her coat a tiny, fluffy, whimpering, flat-black-faced, shiny-nosed, snorting thing. Diane thanked the manager, kissed me, made a 'smooshy smoo' voice to the small object in her arms and headed to the car. "What is it?" I said. The manager shook my hand and replied, "£600 - his father was a champion." "For £600 I want his father to be Muhammad Ali," I retorted, still reeling from a four-hour drive to Wales to pick up our gift of a creature who bore no relation to anything, let alone a dog, that I had ever seen. I coughed up the cash at the renegotiated price of £300 and crunched through the snow to the steamed-up-windowed car. "I thought it was a gift?" Diane, still nuzzling the alien creature, said, "He was, his father was a ...." "I know, I know his father was a champion. What kind of dog is it?" Still smiling, kissing and making cooing noises, Diane said, "a Pekinese. Isn't he cute?" I looked at him; he looked at me. He then sneezed and sprayed my face with puppy snot. I wiped my face with my sleeve. Instead of feeling an instant dislike for this animal, I stared into his Peter Lorre black eyes and reluctantly realised that I had fallen for this creature. "Well?" Diane said. "What shall we call him?" I looked at him. I smiled at my new friend; he smiled back, in a panting kind of way. "Gremlin. His name will be Gremlin."

There are many stories about Gremlin: his first appearance on MTV; his bad behaviour in a scented candle and potpourri shop - leaving new patrons entering with the expression of 'it smells like s**t in here'; the time he fell in love with a visiting Springer Spaniel called Sadie and would not eat for days after she had left – with a subsequent bill from the vet of £50 and a sick note for depression! Then there was the Christmas that Diane accidentally set light to him with a candle - saved by a bottle of Evian and me; his many escapes to the pub in the village where I now live; the various women he introduced me to; and the love he gave me when I was recovering from a car accident. I could have told you of the joy of my little boy Louis calling out Gremlin's name when returning home from nursery; or of our homeopath, Anne, who helped 'Grem' when vets had given up and gave him two more years. When Diane left me I told her she couldn't take Gremlin but she could always visit him, which she did for years.

When Gremlin died it broke my heart.

Sally, my partner, was driving to the station and I was home. The phone rang. I recognised our vet's voice. "Michael, Gremlin died in the night, I'm sorry." I have always thought it strange that when we all get those calls we say, "Thank you". I dialled Sally's mobile. "My dog is dead" I cried.

Sally turned her car around, drove to the vets and returned home with my dog wrapped in his blanket like a baby. She kissed me goodbye and left me with Gremlin in my arms. I have been a lucky man and have loved and been loved, but that morning I cried more for that silly, smelly dog than for any woman. We waited until the weekend to tell the kids - or rather Claudia told us. My little girl, Claudia, was nine and a half and Louis fifteen months younger and their Sunday morning ritual was to snuggle into the foot of our bed and talk, tell stories and laugh, but this morning was different. They sat with the quilt pulled round them. Claudia looked at Sally and I and said, "Grem's not coming back from the vets is he?" That night Louis and I looked out of his bedroom window into the garden beyond the chocolate tree to where Gremlin had been buried, and he asked me, "Do you think Grem will be warm enough out there, Dad?" "He will be sleeping snug in his blanket," I said, trying to hold it together. Sally came into the room and wrapped her arms around both of us.

A few weeks later I found some of Gremlin's toys on his grave.

I asked Louis if he knew anything about it. He said that he had put them there. "Grem might still want to play at night when we are sleeping."

We now have a Parson Jack Russell called Sammy, who is named after a three-legged Westie owned by Claudia's godmother Linda. Sammy is a rescue dog who didn't have a great start to his life. He is not your regular canine and sometimes looks at you like he knows your secrets and understands. Sammy came into our lives a week or so after Sally's father Ron died, and if Ron were a dog he would look like Sam. We also have been adopted by a stray cat, who came into our lives a week after Sally's mum died and we have called her Betty in her memory!

VICKI MICHELLE
ACTRESS

My whole family are animal lovers and we've all had various pets over the years, especially cats and dogs. My favourite would have to be my little Maltese Terrier, Scraffy. He is so funny and such a character. It's amazing how a pet can enhance your life. They really do become one of the family; he even sleeps on the bed. I didn't realise just how much joy he would bring to the house when I bought him for my daughter Louise's tenth birthday. If anyone wakes up a bit grumpy in the morning, you can guarantee it won't be long before he brings a smile to their face, especially when he's playing with his favourite fluffy toy or starts racing round the garden, barking at the planes flying overhead. He thinks he's chasing them off! He really is the best dog in the world.

EMMA MILNE
CELEBRITY VET

People are always asking me what they are. They are a fairly distinctive couple and have been recognised in their own right probably more times than I have. They are the reason that I get out of bed on horrible winter mornings and walk three miles in the pouring rain. They are quite simply the centre of my life and I am boringly obsessed with them.

I have had them for ten years now and I have, over this time, worked out what all the components of them are. We'll start with Badger. He has the coat of a Border Collie, that much is certain. His ears resemble a set of handlebars and are always at half-mast. He has the 'point' of a pointer. He has the eyes of a hawk and can spot a rabbit at several hundred yards. This rabbit, along with all its friends, is very safe because Badger is a New Age man. He loves small furry creatures and all he wants to do is lick their bottoms and simply sit and watch them for as long as is humanly (or doggedly) possible. He has the elegance and speed of a cheetah, and when he changes from fourth gear into fifth he fluidly flattens his body into one beautiful, streamlined vision and turns into a black and white blur. He always has a slightly gormless expression because his mouth is always slightly open with a quizzical look in his eye. He lives and loves to run.

Pan is quite a different creature. He has the eyes of a wolf and when he fixes you with those beautiful, orange eyes he seems to look right inside you. He has the coat of a husky crossed with a bear. He has the high rump and sprinting speed of a thoroughbred racehorse combined with about as much stamina as a man trying to make love after ten pints. Rabbits are safe from him too; not through any caring desire that he has to study them, but simply because he runs about like a headless chicken and doesn't even see most of them. He has the tail of Basil Brush. He has the appetite of a Labrador. He lives and loves to eat and no unguarded bin is safe from him.

Separately they are beautiful, stunning dogs, but together they are a priceless unit. They are completely inseparable. They refuse steadfastly to play with other dogs, and if another dog is running with them they simply ignore it. If it gets in the way of their game they scornfully grumble at it and then resume whatever they were doing. Their favourite pastime is the twig game. Pan will very pointedly find a small twig and hold it very delicately in his teeth and will wait until Badger notices he's got it. If Badger is pretending he hasn't seen him, Pan will run on the spot staring at him and start whining. Badger will then start to run away from him and commence his attack from a wide arc. He will canter until he is within striking distance and directly behind Pan, and then he will change gear and flatten out to full speed. Pan will wait for him and watch him out of the corner of his eye and then duck to one side right at the last minute. Badger will fly past him, teeth snapping wildly in mid-air as he pretends he was really trying to get the stick. This will continue for several attack-cum-runs. At some point Pan will get bored and lie down and just start chewing the twig. Badger will commence his run, but when he realises Pan is not going to run away he will simply start 'springing'. This is another of Badger's particular talents, during which he resembles a slightly gormless antelope with handlebar ears. He springs round Pan in big, four-feet-off-the-floor jumps and wildly snaps his teeth in the air. Pan steadfastly ignores him until the twig is shredded and will then casually get up and saunter off. Badger will stare after him with a disappointed look for several seconds and eventually give up and follow him.

They trot along with a loping gait and are often touching flanks as they go. At some telepathic point, only started by some unique, unseen signal between them, they will run at full speed to a completely empty tree where they once saw a squirrel five months previously and leap repeatedly up at the tree barking wildly. This usually ends when Pan decides for no particular reason to savage Badger playfully in the side of the neck. At this point they will both stop and just stare into the distance for a few seconds and then trot off together. Pan likes to savage Badger in the neck quite frequently for no apparent reason even when there are no invisible squirrels involved. Badger's revenge for this is his particular pièce de résistance. We call it his 'zebra-take-down-manoeuvre'.

It all starts with the dogs leaping about and wrestling like boxing hares. There will be a lot of scruff-pulling and leg-chewing on both parts. At any opportune moment when Pan's rump presents itself, Badger will go for the kill. He seizes a painfully large-looking piece of Pan's flesh on his back. The exact location of this piece of flesh is critical for the manoeuvre to work. It has to be just far enough back for Pan to be unable to turn and reach him and right on top to make it even more difficult. Pan twists and turns and tries to shake him off, but Badger has a lot of savaging to make up for and hangs on in a spirited fashion. Eventually Pan succumbs as a zebra does to a lion and crashes to the floor in an agonising feigned death roll. Badger, victorious, will immediately straddle the prone and upturned Pan and set about him. His point proved, they will then decide to go and look for some small, furry things of one sort or another and trot off amicably, sides touching, tongues lolling and with a very contented air about them.

No matter what mood I am in they always make me smile. They never sulk because I am moody. They are always there to put a head on my knee when I am upset and they can always be relied upon to jump directly and accurately onto your bladder when they are allowed upstairs for a cuddle on special occasions.

So what are they? They are dogs.

LAILA MORSE
ACTRESS

I love my animals. I've got two dogs and a cat: a Jack Russell, a Toy Poodle and a Bengal cat; their names are Eric, Henry and Drexel. They all play together and give us such a lot of fun.

ALBERT MOSES
ACTOR

I love all pets. I had an Alsatian, five cats, bred budgerigars and had a fish tank as well.

My Alsatian was called Charlie and he was very protective of the cats. They used to sleep with him in his basket. Any stranger or another cat or dog approaching them was met with a growl. He played with them, racing about in the garden, and even shared his food.

I trained budgerigars to sit on my shoulder and take food from the corner of my mouth. They flew about freely in the house and never tried to fly out. They could ring a bell by pulling on the string, pull a tiny cart and do zigzag turns round obstacles.

I trained the fish to come up to the top of the tank when I rang a bell. It is amazing what one can teach one's pets.

I miss them all.

RADHA NILLIA &
AYVEE VERZONILLA
SINGERS (US)

We love our puppies, Bella and Jah King, because they remind us of how beautiful life is. Bella and Jah King teach us to enjoy the innocence of everyday abundance. More Peace and Light to all Doggies.

KIRSTEN O'BRIEN
TELEVISION PRESENTER

I was allergic to most things when I was growing up (I probably still am!) so having a pet was out of the question. Also, we travelled around to lots of countries so it would have been a bit of a pet passport palaver. I suppose because of this when I was really little I kept mice made out of cotton wool in a cage, which were really easy to look after although they did moult a bit and their stuck on eyes sometimes fell off! My only proper pet was a goldfish. I won her at Ripon fair and so named her after the then newsreader Angela Rippon. I kept Angela on my windowsill in my bedroom and fed her diligently but got into trouble when my mum suggested she might need her water changing. Being an inventive child (I refer you back to the mice!) I decided that Angela just needed a freshen up and to my shame I popped in a few drops of my perfume. Luckily my mum saved the day and Angela was plopped into our mixing bowl whilst mum hastily changed the water. She survived and lived out her days on my windowsill. I should add that I now keep fish and am very thorough with the cleaning – oh, and mum's cakes always tasted a bit funny after that day.

TOM O'CONNOR
TELEVISION PRESENTER & COMEDIAN

Apart from hamsters and fish, the only family pet is our eight-year-old Pekinese. He's a great guard dog, very loyal, intelligent and extremely clean (more like a cat than a dog). I take him on the course with me and he's also a great golf ball finder.

NICK OWEN
TELEVISION PRESENTER

I am an unashamed cat lover, having had five of them during my adult life. I think they are remarkably graceful creatures, mysterious and sometimes remote, but never too far away. A friend of mine once said that dogs live FOR you, cats live WITH you - probably quite true.

I have experience of dogs too, including a beautiful white Labrador called Suzie, who was absolutely wonderful with our then small children. She was an integral part of the family until she was cruelly struck down by a speeding driver in thick snow outside our house before my very eyes. A dreadful memory - it was half past ten at night and the noise of the impact woke the children. We were all shattered. Love her as I did, I have to say I am still drawn more to cats; particularly Freddie, a ginger tom, who is on his last legs as I write.

Freddie has been around for a major portion of our two younger children's lives, Chris and Jenny. He's getting on for fourteen now and becoming more and more affectionate by the day. You only have to sit down and he's on your lap in a flash. He's nearly always outside the front door waiting for us when we drive home. He has a habit of popping up in unexpected little places and we are constantly saying to each other, "Just look at Freddie," as he gets himself into some wonderful positions of relaxation. In fact they are wonderfully relaxing creatures to have around. He's undoubtedly more clingy as his health deteriorates. By the time you read this, he'll have gone and we'll miss him terribly.

It's so difficult with pets, isn't it? You can love them so much, but feel so desolate if anything happens to them. Children can be inconsolable and you sometimes wonder if it's worth the pain. But I am certain it is. Children learn how to love another creature, how to care for them and how to cope with grief - all part of real life. I know that Freddie, and all our other pets, have vastly enriched the texture of our lives. But dear, dear Freddie, we are going to miss you so much.

CHRIS PACKHAM
TELEVISION PRESENTER

Here's a poem I wrote a little while ago when I wasn't too happy. I am forever indebted to my two mad mates because they very seriously kept me going when stopping was the longed for option. For thus and so much more they are everything to me.

The Joy of Running

I can laugh at one thing and that is them just running .
Big running when they just go horizon chasing and run to vanish
from me
When they go from balls to spots to dust to pinprick black and gone .
And then there's nothing but the wind and rain
and the churning grass
or the dull sand
and me squinting .
And then the run rewinds and they rocket back , bucking and
bounding ,
galloping head down back to me . Back to me .
They come back to me .
They bicker , hang around , the drizzle tickles their backs and . . . go. .
.

And I always laugh more as they are running away
at the sheer joy of their just running .
And I wish I could run away .
Vanish.
Go.
And not come back to me .

I know it's a bit . . . but at least it's honest .

JULIE PEASGOOD
ACTRESS & TELEVISION PRESENTER

Our cat Wesley is the pet I loved more than any other. He had an unfortunate habit of sunbathing in the middle of the road, which in the end was the reason for his untimely death, but he was so trusting and affectionate - even the hardest of souls couldn't pass him on the tarmac without bending down for a furtive stroke.

Wesley didn't actually realise he was a cat. He would bobble down the road, following us with the enthusiasm of a small terrier - and then when the terrain took him out of his comfort zone he would sit (or sunbathe) patiently for ages until myself or my husband, Patrick, finally hoved into view. And he would then consider it his job to escort us safely back home.

Wesley possessed an iron bladder - we often took him down to our cottage in Cornwall and he would never complain for the entire four to five-hour journey. I don't think we ever witnessed him having a poo; in fact he certainly never had any accidents - he was far too proud!

The only fault Wes had (except we didn't see it as such) was that he had the appetite of a small horse. We actually found his ravenous hunger quite endearing, but the rest of our road didn't share our sentiments. It was only at the end, when we were searching for him, that we discovered from neighbours that he used to hoover up every other animal's food (as well as his own) and I know Patrick still doesn't forgive himself for putting him on Science Diet rations to cure his enormous belly.

We miss him so much. His eccentricity, his smell, his bravery, and the way he'd very, very gently bite your nose when he wanted to show you how grateful he was. We were so lucky to enjoy him - and we'll never ever forget him.

SARAH PRESTON
ACTRESS

Oscar, my eight-year-old Boxer dog. My entire world revolves around him ... where I go, he goes. He's sensitive yet brave; strong yet incredibly gentle; well behaved yet wilful; an old soul yet playful. He is my joy, my light, my soulmate ....

SHEILA REID
ACTRESS

As a child there was Schooner, a golden-haired, silky-eared Cocker Spaniel. Always smiling, he would bound back quivering with excitement to wait for me when I daydreamed and dawdled on family walks.

Then, grown-up pets. First, Thomas the Magnificent, Emperor of cats. Half Abyssinian and named after Alfie Lynch's wonderful performance as Sir Thomas Moore in A Man for All Seasons. "You've called your cat Tom - how original!" people would say. My gardening companion - he would drape himself across my shoulders like a soft fur stole.

And after: Paz and Lola - half Somali brother and sister. He, fearless and spiritual, handsome and loving, would share in my yoga and meditation; and she, skittish and shy by turns, fastidious, adorable and pretty as paint.

All adored and bringing huge joy.

ALISA REYES
ACTRESS (US)

My number one favourite pet at the moment is my very own cat Bootsy. She is a black and white Tux cat with white boots. Go figure on the name! I used to own two rabbits, Kiki and Thumper, and a Maine Coon cat named Bitsy.

I love cats and rabbits because they are so lovable and caring. Cats are very easy to take care of. Rabbits, on the other hand, are a bit more challenging. But if you are patient then they are the animals for you. I also adore dogs. I love teacups or anything small that you can fit in a purse.

As far as a wild animals go, I love elephants. As regards water animals, I love dolphins.

MAISIE SMITH
ACTRESS

I have two Jack Russell's called Benny and Betty. They are 2 years old and very cute. When I watch the telly they love to lay on my lap and lick me or fall asleep. My dogs love a cuddle!

SAMIA SMITH
ACTRESS

My favourite pet is my dog, Sonny. He is a Maltese Terrier and spoilt rotten! We got him when he was ten weeks old and he has been a major part of the family from day one. He has a great personality, is really loving and is very cheeky! Considering he is only a small dog he demands more walks than a Labrador, so he keeps us really fit!

I think the saying that 'a dog is a man's best friend' couldn't be more true. I think having a pet enriches your life, so I would recommend it to anyone!

JOHN STAPLETON
TELEVISION PRESENTER

I have been a cat man for as long as I can remember. They have all been moggies. Big, fat and spoilt, they have lived a life of feline luxury because when it comes to cats I am a pathetically soft touch.

The first was Snooky, grey and white but frequently black as well because, for reasons I never understood, she loved to go into the coal shed. In those days we lived in the Pennines outside Manchester where Snooky enjoyed not just the food put down for her in the kitchen but also a wide variety of wildlife. Like most of our cats she lived to a ripe old age and we missed her terribly curled up in a ball by the fireside.

When my wife Lynn and I first got together we took in Mutt and Geoff. Mutt, a scallywag of a cat and the runt of the litter, we adopted because we knew no one else would. Geoff we took because he was pretty but rather timid.

Fudge was the only feline tragedy we have had. By now our son Nick had entered our lives and we took in Fudge, a gorgeous tabby, along with Squeaky, an equally attractive black female so named because - guess what - she squeaked! One Easter weekend we got a got a call from a distressed motorist who confessed that he had just run over and killed Fudge. Nick, just six at the time, was distraught. It was his first bereavement and he wanted to know every detail of the circumstances in which Fudge had died and where he would be buried.

By way of therapy we bought a lookalike - the white-pawed Socks who even now, fifteen years later, is still Nick's cat, demonstrating for him a much greater affection than either of us enjoy.

Squeaky is decidedly mine largely because, I am ashamed to admit, she knows that all she has to do is to look at me with her big doey eyes, squeak once or twice, and she will be fed. Yes, I know I shouldn't. I know I should be cruel to be kind. But as I said at the start, I am at heart a big softie.

JASON STEVENS
TELEVISION PRESENTER, SPEAKER & AUTHOR

My favourite pet was a dog named Chocky. He was never fussed about anything, and although he was small he would defend our house as though he was the size of a Great Dane. Chocky was unlike the dog we had before that, Bluey.

Bluey would chase motorcycles and try to bite their tyres. One day he knocked over a bikie. My brother and I saw it and did the bolt; in fact my brother ran so fast that he jumped over a fence and fell, breaking his arm. We were only young and we thought that because he was a bikie he would be mad - he wasn't; he actually was a very nice person and didn't even charge us for the damage Bluey did to the bike from causing it to fall.

LANA TAILOR
ACTRESS & MODEL (Canada)

My favourite pet has always been a dog, as they have their own unique personalities. They are also very loyal, loving and playful! I'd have to say that my all-time favourite dog is a Bichon Maltese.

Growing up, I had a Bichon named Pebbles who was a part of the family. Though she had several medical problems, her resilience was absolutely astonishing! She was a very strong dog!

HAYLEY TAMADDON
ACTRESS

His name is Ozzy, and he's a very handsome two-year-old Shih-tzu who absolutely loves his mummy! Two years ago, as I was just about to leave Emmerdale, my fiancé Darren was also going to work in China for three months. I thought, oh great - no job, and my boyfriend is going away! I will be so lonely! So Darren said he would buy me a puppy to keep me company (and to shut me up, as I'd been begging to have a dog for ages).

The minute I met Ozzy I fell in love with him. I have never seen anything so cute in my life! I took him home and he slept next to me all night, like a baby. The following day I received a phone call from my agent saying I had got the lead role in the musical The Rocky Horror Show and in two weeks (!) I would be starting a tour around the UK for four months! There was me thinking I probably wouldn't get another job for ages!

But what about Ozzy?! I couldn't possibly give him back - I'd already fallen in love with him. So there was only one thing I could do: train him and take him on tour with me!

I bought puppy-training books, toys, treats, and the best thing ever invented for a dog - PUPPY PADS! In two weeks Ozzy learned to sit, lie down, beg, wait, fetch, leave … and where to do his wee-wees! And I'm proud to say I did it all on my own.

So there we were, me and my best friend, on the road - on tour! He came everywhere with me - to every theatre, and every hotel - and he was as good as gold. People would say, "Wow, he is so well behaved! And so intelligent!" And I'd be like: "That's my boy!"

Two years on and Ozzy is doing great. He is so clever and funny and, as stupid as this sounds, I'm sure he understands me when I talk to him! Sometimes if I'm sad or upset he will come and lie next to me and nuzzle his face into mine, like he's saying, "Don't worry, mummy, I'll give you a cuddle." And when I'm getting ready to go out, knowing he'll have to stay at home on his own, the minute he hears the hairdryer or sees me getting dressed he hides under the sofa! How clever is that?

My life wouldn't be the same without Ozzy. He brings me so

much joy and laughter. He only has to look at me with those big brown eyes and my heart melts. I just don't understand how people can be cruel to animals; it makes me so upset and angry. Animals have hearts, they have thoughts, just like we do; they cry just like we do and they feel pain just like we do.

If I ever see a dog roaming the streets, I have to stop the car and go see if it's okay, and if it's wearing a dog tag I take it home. Once I ended up with a huge Alsatian in my back garden! Well, I couldn't leave it wandering the streets, could I? So I took it to the vets and luckily it was microchipped.

I love animals, all animals. I have a huge passion for horses and ride at least three times a week; one day soon I will buy my own. But no one will ever take the place of 'my favourite pet'. That is - and always will be - My OZZY xxx

GABRIEL THOMSON
ACTOR

I don't have a favourite pet (as they might get jealous), though I do have a slightly deranged Burmese cat named Wacky and a lovely gentle Lurcher whom we rescued from Battersea Dogs Home called Stan.

JANE TONKS
TELEVISION PRESENTER

Teddy (Bengal) died in 2008 from cancer and is sorely missed, as he was our first baby before we had our kids. He was much loved and really did have nine lives, as he went missing in Ealing, London, only to turn up in Richmond nine weeks later, fatter than ever - he was so friendly that everybody was feeding him! RIP Tedskie.

LAUREN VAKNINE
RADIO PRESENTER & BROADCASTER

When I was three years old I came home from nursery one day to find a beautiful German Shepherd puppy waiting for me in my kitchen. My dad told me that she was a rescue dog and that by taking her we had saved her. At the time I was into a cartoon that featured a dog named Scruffy, so I decided to call her Scruffy (how unoriginal!) Scruffy was an amazing dog to have around as a child, as she kept me company, looked out for me and, because I had arthritis from the age of two, helped me get around and would sit at the end of the sofa so I could put my feet up on her – how understanding dogs can be of our feelings.

However, my mum got pregnant with my sister and was still working full-time and therefore decided that having such a big dog was not an option anymore, so after only a year of having Scruffy in our lives we let her go to a lovely lady who lived on a farm in Chester. I cried for days after she left, but my parents assured me that she would be very happy being able to run around a big farm with other dogs, as opposed to being stuck in our small house in London.

For years after that I pestered my mum for another dog. She would dread going past a pet shop because I would beg to go in and see the puppies, but she very rarely let me as she knew how upset I would be once I had seen the puppies and then received a firm 'NO' from her.

A few years ago my cousin got a long-haired Dachshund called Slinky and I fell in love with him. He had the most wonderful nature and was beautiful. I was having a very bad arthritis flare-up and my cousin asked if I wanted Slinky to come over to keep me company during the days when they were at work, and after my parents agreed, he came round. He kept me company the way Scruffy used to and it was wonderful. Even if we did nothing, he would sit on my lap while I watched TV – just him being there made me feel better. My parents could see how he made me feel and how well I cared for him – when my cousin went away Slinky stayed with us for a week – so they agreed to let me have another dog as long as I took on the responsibility myself.

So I took myself down to 'Discover Dogs' at Earls Court to see all the different breeds there were. I knew I had to get a small dog because our house isn't that big and I didn't want to have to walk him for hours every day so I had a few in mind, but as I walked in I saw a young girl walking the most stunning dog I'd ever seen, so I asked her what breed he was. She told me he was a German Spitz Klein and there were about fifteen of them there today. After walking round the whole venue to see all the more popular breeds, I finally came to the plot that had 'German Spitz' written above it. I saw that there were two types of German Spitz – Klein and Mittel, Kleins being smaller than Mittels. They come from the same family as Pomeranians and in fact used to be called Victorian Pomeranians because Queen Victoria had them. I fell in love with all of them and got some numbers of breeders.

Later that week I went up to the Cotswolds to meet Gloria, a lady who had been breeding German Spitzen for sixty years, and there I met the most wonderful puppy I had ever seen. He was seven weeks old at the time and I wanted to have him straight away but had to wait until he had had all his vaccinations. Two weeks later I went to pick up my puppy, whom I called Milo.

I have now had Milo for nine months and he has brought more joy to my life than I ever thought possible for an animal to bring! Not only do I get stopped everywhere I go with people asking about him, but also he keeps me company and sits with me when I am unwell. He has changed my lifestyle because we now go to the park daily and have met lots of other dog owners whom we now walk with every day and it does us both good to get some regular exercise! When I walk in the door after being out there is not a time when he is not happy to see me, and the love and affection he shows are indescribable.

Dogs love their owners unconditionally; all they ask for is food, water, some exercise and a lot of love and caring. I could not imagine my life without Milo now and neither can my family – even though they were reluctant to get him in the first place. I have heard that people who have dogs are less likely to have heart problems and now I can understand this. Aside from the fact that they make you live a healthier lifestyle, you can be as angry as anything but the minute you see your dog you just can't be angry anymore and this must help the heart! There's nothing like Puppy Love!

JEREMY WADE
TRAVEL/FISHING WRITER &
TELEVISION PRESENTER

My favourite pet is my brother's dog, Larry. From a distance he looks like a black Lab, but close up he's got wiry hair and a beard and a bit of a Mohican crest - inherited from his mother's side, a Schnauzer. All the neighbours and their kids want to take him for walks, while other people's dogs get fat and ignored. It's something about how interested he is in the world every time he goes out - he lifts my mood, whatever worries and stresses I may have going on.

DAWN WALTERS
ACTRESS (US)

My cat, Pchła (pronounced similar to 'Pwa'), is very special. He was born on a farm and given to me as a gift when I was teaching English in Poland. His name means 'flea'. He has lived in three countries, and when he flew to America the pilot gave him wings to pin on his collar.

Pchła has an extremely curious personality – even for a cat – and is (thankfully) also blessed with many more than nine lives. His most harrowing experience to date has been getting closed in under the bathroom floor by a repairman.

His purr makes me smile and I love him very much.

MICHELLE WATT
TELEVISION PRESENTER

My favourite pet is my current little kitten, PJ (which, in his case, doesn't actually stand for pyjamas!) I liked the name Panther and my husband liked the name Jay, so we gave him a posh double-barrelled name, Panther-Jay and we call him PJ for short (as Panther-Jay wouldn't exactly help his street cred!)

We got him when he was only seven weeks old and he's the centre of attention in our house. He's now nine months old and he's a great little companion to have around. He's unbelievably affectionate and is like my shadow. Where I go, he goes! My hubby and I adore him. I have to confess that I've babied him since he first arrived. He actually lies upside down in my arms like a newborn and would sleep like that for hours if I let him (except my arms start to ache after ten minutes!)

I'm sure I sound biased, but he's honestly such a clever little thing. I've managed to train him like you'd train a dog! He sits to order and even gives a paw in exchange for treats. My friends and family were in disbelief watching him perform his tricks (clearly, I have too much time on my hands!)

I've had other cats in the past, but never one with a personality like PJ. He sure is one of a kind!

GEORGE WATTS
TELEVISION PRESENTER

For me, the most important pet to cherish is the one from your childhood, and in my case this was a four-legged furry friend who joined me on many an adventure! My pet cat Smokey was a curious thing and together we made a top team of explorers, getting up to all kinds of mischief on a daily basis. I can remember escaping into the fields near my family home and together we would hunt out wildlife and make all manner of new discoveries.

Smokey shaped my imagination and became a constant companion as we grew up together. I would not have swapped my childhood buddy for anything!

AMY WEBER
ACTRESS & MODEL

I love my dog Bella. She is a sensitive little thing, but she always knows when I am down and she knows exactly what to do to cheer me up. Dogs have this amazing way of knowing when you need them and they never let you down. I can cry on her shoulder or laugh at her crazy antics. Her smiles and licks make all the white dog hair on my clothes worthwhile!

DENISE WELCH
ACTRESS

My favourite pet was my Labrador, Howard, whom I got when I was at drama school and living with my boyfriend. We called him Howard because that was the name of the character he played in a film. Howard had a wonderful, lovable nature and was always so pleased to see you, even if you had only been out for a short while.

As we started getting more work, it became harder to look after him and so I took him to my parents who became so attached to him. My father, Vin, sold sweets made by the family business and he used to take Howard to his calls in his car. Howard would get out and sniff around but never ran away. Many of the shopkeepers used to invite Howard in and give him a sweet and he became as regular a visitor as my dad!

A few years later I met and married my husband, Tim Healy, who took to Howard as soon as they met. The local TV company, Tyne-Tees Television, asked Tim if he would do a series of programmes called Tim's Travels, which involved Tim going to local music festivals and busking with his guitar. It was Tim's idea to take Howard with him and so he became a bit of a TV star as well. The opening caption was 'Tim's Travels featuring Healy and Howard'. He even got fan mail addressed to 'Tim and Howard'!

He was everyone's favourite and all children who saw him loved him. Happy memories!

ANN WIDDECOMBE
MP

In the course of six decades I have had many cats, all with their own little ways and special characteristics, but perhaps the most memorable has been Monty. I was ten when he arrived.

I had been begging my parents for a cat, but they steadily refused because we had a dog, Tim, and my father believed animals should be obtained at the same time to avoid jealousy. Then one evening my brother arrived home with Monty, a small smoky kitten, in the saddlebag of his bicycle, whom he had rescued from a chicken farm.

He got on famously with the dog from day one and Tim became very protective. If anyone told Monty off, Tim would growl menacingly. Meanwhile he became great friends with the cat from a nearby cottage called Fluffer and the two would go off mousing together with their tails waving side by side.

Two years later we moved to Bath and for some time after Fluffer used to come to our old house and sit waiting sadly for Monty. We took Monty to the new house the night before we moved in and shut him in a room with the window firmly secured by two different catches. However, the following day we arrived to find the window open and Monty gone. He had released both catches, pushed open the window and jumped from the first floor. Who says cats are less intelligent than dogs?

Distraught, we left the removal men to it and combed the surrounding countryside calling "Monty! Monty!" Our shouts fell on deaf ears and we returned mournfully to the new house. Then, long after I was in bed, he walked nonchalantly up the garden path, located the kitchen with unerring instinct and demanded food.

The room in which he had been confined was my bedroom and each night he would come in and perform his Houdini trick with the window. He rarely went out until gone midnight and meanwhile would snuggle down beside me, purring contentedly. We never did work out how he got back, but in the morning he was always there on the bed.

He was a terrific hunter and I would often be asked by my

more squeamish mother to remove mice and voles from the house, but once he brought home a pheasant and our admiration knew no bounds.

Alas, one of his catches poisoned him and he died after a short illness. We did not get another cat for a few years. Somehow it seemed disrespectful to replace Monty.

TIM WILLCOX
NEWS PRESENTER

I happen to be a big fan of sheep. We have five breeding ewes - Shetlands - on a small water meadow near our house in Oxfordshire. This year they produced nine lambs, four girls and five boys, which we are going to eat. No names, since we eat them, but great education as far as animal husbandry, lambing, etc., goes for the children.

Our pet inside the house is Claude, a moggy, who is a fearless killer, often taking on rabbits larger than himself. It makes for some quite gruesome early mornings in the kitchen!

LUCY WILLIAMSON
ACTRESS & SINGER

I have had pets for as long as I can remember. At my family home, growing up we always had Toy Poodles; first Sophie, then Poppy and Holly. I now live in my own house with my own Toy Poodle, Daisy-Boo.

It never ceases to amaze me how much joy pets, and animals in general, bring to people. I certainly view my dog as my best friend and, regardless of what I do, she is always there, seeming to understand me.

Poodles are fantastic as they do not shed hair, and it is extremely rare for someone to be allergic to them because of this. Every Poodle we as a family have ever owned has had the most fantastic temperament. They are intelligent, caring, fun-loving and absolutely fabulous around babies and children.

I am a big animal lover and feel we should all take the time to give our pets as much joy and love as they, without question, give us.

ANNIE WOOD
ACTRESS (US)

I adore my Maltese-cross pup, Lucy, who, though only ten inches tall, has both a huge personality and a huge place in our lives. Although home is Los Angeles, Lucy goes everywhere on location (and vacation!) with her Mamma and Papa, so she is a much travelled little dog with lots of air miles to her credit! She has her own blog on the web and has even started to write a novel, "Woofin' It!" Recently we have been travelling in Europe both for work and pleasure - you may like to read this extract from Lucy's recent entries on the blog, where she woofs about her travelling experiences!

"I had my humans carry my stuff again. They really are quite accommodating. Both of them schlepped (schlepping - Yiddish for carrying a bunch of stuff and oy! it's such a pain in the tuchas!) several bags on and off trains, cabs, planes and finally onto the boat today. Mamma and Papa seem pretty pooped. I, on the other hand, spent my day resting comfortably in my lovely bag surrounded by my favourite toys, enjoying a gentle buzz from a dropper full of Bach Remedy. Right, they wish! I cried on the plane and even let out a bark or two. They should have given me more of that stuff. What do you want from me? It's a bag. I'm claustrophobic. It's probably a past-life fear thing. Maybe I'll see someone about it upon my return to the States."

KEVIN WOODFORD
CELEBRITY CHEF

Say hello to Frankie!

Having been 'looked after' by my dog Plum, a cross Labrador/Spaniel, for many years, I simply couldn't bear the thought of having a new owner after she died, and then along came Frankie! Albeit that he belongs to my daughter, he, along with my son's Labradoodle, Jeffrey, has brought the laughter lines back into my face.

ALASTAIR YATES
NEWS PRESENTER

My Golden Retriever is called Mimpi. Everyone she meets wants to know about her unusual name. It comes from the words Mimpi Indah, which is Balinese for Sweet Dreams. My dog's pedigree name includes 'sweet' in her title and so with my memories of that magical island she was given this mysterious name.

Like most of her breed, she adores water and loves to have a dip in the sea. However, unlike her peers, Mimpi is a gourmet diner: she will leave a bowl of food all day until some speciality from our plates has been added ... or until someone joins her to dine!

She has the typical trait of being placid, but one thing in life can really drive her to distraction: the squirrels in my garden. She's never managed to catch one though!

XIXI YANG
ACTRESS & TV HOST (US)

Growing up in a traditional Chinese family where the first nursery rhyme I learned was 'Mice Stole Rice, Cat Ate Mice', I was not a huge fan of rodents. I remember my grandma roaming around the small kitchen in between meals with huge cans of pesticides, screaming "Ayaaa! Shoo, shoo!" at the top of her lungs, chasing away the smirking mice as they returned to their homes with food. I would then take the cue, put down my homework books, tiptoe into the next room, and sneak online to play Pokemon. As far as I was concerned, anything that motivated my grandma to run around for 20 minutes, after which she would immediately nap for a few hours at a time, was nothing but genius! I didn't care much about rodents at that time, but they sure took care of my well-being!

In high school I met my best friend, Justine, who introduced me to the world of unique pets. Justine is quite the opposite of me - highly intelligent, eccentric, and a bit of an introvert. Instead of going to mundane Friday night football games and gawking at Johnny's most recent muscle developments, Justine would always convince me that we should entertain ourselves with what we thought as a higher, more meaningful source of fun. So when Friday nights rolled around, we would do things like update our MySpace pages or play with her pets.

While I was still new to the world of petdom, Justine was already an expert at taking care of three different types of animals in her room - mice, guinea pigs and a snake. I'm not one to object to having crazy pets, but having both rodents and reptiles as pets, where one species of animal could possibly feed off the other species, was pretty entertaining. Justine would not hear of such a ridiculous idea.

"Do you want to hold her?" Justine asked me the first time I met her pets, petting the little guinea pig on her back as she ran around the inside of Justine's palm.

"No."

"Here you go!" Mistaking my "no" for a "yes", Justine handed me the tiny creature anyway. I felt her furry little body roll all over my hands, tickling my nerves with her nails. Then, all of a sudden, a warm puddle of yellowish liquid began to form under the little rodent's body.

"Yuck! I think she peed on me." My hands shook, and the guinea pig quickly jumped back down to her cage for security.

"Stop it, you scared her! She never urinates on human hands unless she's nervous," Justine reasoned as she picked up the guinea pig and did a mouth-to-nose kiss. "You're okay now, don't worry," she said to her beloved furry friend.

I always wondered how Justine could be so loving to her mice, guinea pigs and snake. I must admit though, the cuteness and harmlessness of those creatures grew on me and I secretly envied the love, comfort and companionship she received from her little friends.

The summer I moved to Los Angeles, CA, from New York City to further my career as a TV host and an actress, I decided to try out the lifestyle myself by getting a few furry friends in my new apartment. After wandering around pet shops at random for a few days, looking for small and friendly pets that are easy to take care of, I settled on two adorable guinea pigs! One is half brown, half white, and moves about two feet in total a day, named Coco, and the other one is half white, half black, with round, chubby cheeks, named Trekkie.

The moment I met Coco and Trekkie, I fell in love with them, and they fell in love with me - or at least whenever I had treats in my hands! Justine has always told me that in a healthy, successful pet/owner relationship, the pet and the owner have to choose one another. I have never been so emotionally vulnerable in my whole life as when I held the two soft, furry babies in my hands. They were my babies! That split second I promised to do whatever it takes to provide them with a comfortable, loving environment and protect them from the world.

As I walked out of the animal store that day, I had to restrain myself from fighting with the cashier in that my two adorable babies were not 'items' and should not be listed along the same columns as Vitamin C drops and dried fruits!

After about a week of getting to know each other, Coco and Trekkie quickly became sisters! Coco was the daredevil and Trekkie was the scaredy-cat. Trekkie would always follow Coco as they roamed around my living room, exploring from one corner to another, leaving their trail of bullets behind. They were also both city girls. They preferred the outdoor environment - with cars honking, birds chirping, and the most suitable view for people-watching from my balcony - from being inside a room. Whenever I would approach their cage, they would eagerly run up to me and bob their heads up and down, as if I were holding seeds in my hands. Whenever I held out strands of Timothy hay, they would always crowd over my fingers and nibble the strands right out of my palm. The happiness and joy expressed on their beady eyes were enough to capture my heart.

For once in my life, I'm a proud mama of two!

My grandmother from China still cannot believe that in America and other Western countries people have rodents as pets! I personally think that exotic animals such as guinea pigs are the best! They are adorable, cuddly and extremely friendly. Coco and Trekkie have brought me countless precious moments in my life. Their sincerity and loyal attitude were more than enough to help me through the toughest times. Don't be fooled by the small packages they come in! Guinea pigs carry an abundance of love and dreams for the future! While Trekkie was having her brunch the other morning, she secretly told me that she wants to audition for Disney's G-Force 2 this fall!